LEADING
WOMEN

Golda Meir

JEAN F. BLASHFIELD

Marshall Cavendish
Benchmark
New York

Other Marshall Cavendish Offices:
Marshall Cavendish International (Asia) Private Limited, 1 New Industrial Road, Singapore 536196 • Marshall Cavendish International (Thailand) Co Ltd., 253 Asoke, 12th Flr., Sukhumvit 21 Road, Klongtoey Nua, Wattana, Bangkok 10110, Thailand • Marshall Cavendish (Malaysia) Sdn Bhd, Times Subang, Lot 46, Subang Hi-Tech Industrial Park, Batu Tiga, 40000 Shah Alam, Selangor Darul Ehsan, Malaysia

Marshall Cavendish is a trademark of Times Publishing Limited.
All websites were available and accurate when this book was sent to press.

Library of Congress Cataloging-in-Publication Data
Blashfield, Jean F.
Golda Meir / by Jean F. Blashfield.
p. cm. — (Leading women)
Summary: "Presents the biography of Golda Meir against the backdrop of her political, historical, and cultural environment"—Provided by publisher.
Includes bibliographical references and index.
ISBN 978-0-7614-4960-7
1. Meir, Golda, 1898-1978—Juvenile literature.
2. Women prime ministers—Israel—Biography—Juvenile literature.
3. Prime ministers—Israel—Biography—Juvenile literature.
4. Israel—Biography—Juvenile literature. I. Title.
DS126.6.M42B53 2010
956.9405'3092—dc22 [B]
2009030630
Editor: Deborah Grahame   Art Director: Anahid Hamparian
Publisher: Michelle Bisson   Series Designer: Nancy Sabato
Photo research by Connie Gardner

Cover photo by Hulton Archive/Getty Images
The photographs in this book are used by permission and through the courtesy of: *Getty Images*: AFP, 1, 70, 86; Hulton Archive, 10, 54, 67, 92; Getty Images Europe, 31, 44, 63, 83; Popperfoto; 50; Time and Life, 58; *The Image Works*: Manuel Bidemanas, 100; *Corbis*: Hulton Deutsch Collection, 4; Alfredo Dagli Orti, 27; Bettmann, 38; Underwood and Underwood, 40; *Art Resource*: Reunion des Musees Nationaux, 9; *Milwaukee Public Library*: 12, 14; *AP Photo*: 16, 24, 78; Jim Pringle, 75.

Printed in Malaysia (T)
135642

CONTENTS

CHAPTER 1

From Russia to Milwaukee 4

CHAPTER 2

Finding Her Voice 12

CHAPTER 3

The Land She Meant to Tame 24

CHAPTER 4

Working Her Way Up 40

CHAPTER 5

Making a Nation 50

CHAPTER 6

World War II and the United Nations 58

CHAPTER 7

Working for Her New Country 70

CHAPTER 8

Golda as Foreign Minister 78

CHAPTER 9

A New Life 86

CHAPTER 10

The Prime Minister 92

CHAPTER 11

The Last Days 100

TIMELINE 104
SOURCE NOTES 106
FURTHER INFORMATION 108
BIBLIOGRAPHY 109
INDEX 110

CHAPTER ONE

From Russia to Milwaukee

HER EARLIEST MEMORIES WERE OF FEAR—fear and trembling at the panicky whispering of her parents, and hammering as her father nailed boards across the door of her home. She didn't understand what it was all about, but she later found out that her family had been preparing for an attack by anti-Semitic Cossacks. It was an attack that didn't come, at least not at that time. But that fear ever after played in little Golda Mabovitch's mind as she helped to build a homeland where Jews would be free from hate-driven attacks. She couldn't have dreamed that her personal story would also be the story of Israel, the nation that became the Jewish homeland.

Little Goldie, as everyone called her, stood apart from her neighbors in the Russian city of Kiev. Other children her age, who might otherwise have been playmates, ignored her. Golda recalled,

> I remember being aware that this was happening to me because I was Jewish, which made me different from most of the other children. . . . It was a feeling that I was to know again many times during my life—the fear, the frustration, the consciousness of being different and the profound instinctive belief that if one wanted to survive, one had to take effective action about it personally.

The Cossacks were fighters who attacked Jews in Russia, where young Golda lived.

Who was attacking the Jews in Kiev, and why were they doing it? In the late 1800s, a kind of anti-Jewish sentiment called anti-Semitism began to develop. (Although the Semitic peoples include Jews, Arabs, and many others, the term *anti-Semitism* has come to refer only to animosity toward Jews.)

It became fashionable to be proudly anti-Semitic. People based their hatred of the Jews on religion—some Christians regarded Jews as "Christ killers." In czarist Russia, leaders justified the killing of Jews by citing the incorrect belief that the Jews used the blood of baby Christians to make matzo, the unleavened bread eaten particularly at the important Jewish holiday of Passover. Anti-Jewish riots, called pogroms, became a kind of sport for some people. Such terrifying pogroms were among Golda's earliest memories of life in Kiev.

Russians had persecuted Jews since the reign of Catherine the Great in the late 1700s. Catherine and subsequent czars promoted anti-Semitism because it redirected the anger of the people from the monarchy toward Jewish scapegoats. Fighters called Cossacks became one of the most rabid groups of anti-Semites. These warriors fought sometimes with, other times against, the czar.

Catherine decreed that Jews must live in a region called the Pale of Settlement. Starting about 1880, Christian attacks on Jews in the Pale increased. Marauding Cossacks led most of the attacks. These bands of militant Christians on horseback often barreled through the streets of the towns and slashed their swords at anyone who might be Jewish. These are the events that Goldie remembered from her earliest childhood.

Moshe Yitzhak Mabovitch, Goldie's father, had been allowed to live outside the Pale, in Kiev (now in Ukraine). He gained this right because he was a superb cabinetmaker. Moshe's great skill did not guarantee a good living, however, and the family was very poor.

Moshe and his wife, Blume, first had a daughter, Sheyna. Later, Blume had five sons, none of whom lived more than a year. Then Golda, strong and eager to live, arrived on May 3, 1898. The Mabovitches' youngest child was another daughter, Tzipka, or Zipporah (later called Clara). She was four years younger than Goldie.

Goldie had a mind of her own, so much so that some relatives were convinced that she was possessed by a dybbuk—a malicious spirit of Eastern European folklore. Because Goldie was so independent, she usually was allowed to wander at will, while Blume took care of Tzipka.

Goldie followed her adored older sister, Sheyna, wherever the teenager went. Often staying hidden, Goldie would listen as Sheyna and her friends talked about politics. "Down with the czar!" she heard them say. Sheyna could have been imprisoned for expressing such a thought in public.

In these conversations, Goldie first heard the idea of a homeland for the Jews—a place where they would no longer be a hated minority. Depending on which friends Sheyna was close with at any particular time, Goldie watched her sister move back and forth between Zionism and socialism. The Zionists thought that the Jews could solve their problems by moving to the Promised Land offered by God. The socialists, on the other hand, wanted to turn Russia into a

WHO ARE JEWS, AND WHAT IS JUDAISM?

Judaism is the religion of the Jews. They are descendants of the biblical figure Abraham and his followers, who lived almost four thousand years ago. The book of Genesis in the Hebrew Bible says that God spoke to Abraham and chose him to father a nation if he would make solemn agreement, or covenant, to recognize God as the single supreme deity. Until that time, people generally believed that many different gods inhabited the world around them and played roles in their lives. Two other great religions, both recognizing a single God, also spread through Abraham's descendants. They are Christianity and Islam.

Abraham probably lived in Babylon (now part of Iraq) and eventually, with his wife Sarah, settled in Canaan, which probably was located about where Israel is today. Sarah was unable to bear children, so she gave Abraham permission to father a child with her maid, Hagar. Hagar's son, Ishmael, was already several years old when Sarah succeeded in having a son, named Isaac. Sarah insisted that Abraham send Hagar and Ishmael away into the wilderness.

The Arab people trace their heritage to Ishmael and his twelve sons, though the religion of Islam, followed by most Arabs today, was not established until the birth of the prophet Muhammad in the 600s CE. Jews trace their heritage to Isaac and his two sons, Jacob and Esau. Jacob's name was later changed to Israel. Thus, the Jews are called sons of Israel. Israel himself fathered twelve sons, each of whom founded one of the twelve tribes of Israel. One tribe is called the Tribe of Judah, from which the word *Judaism* stems.

According to the Bible, an angel told Sarah and Abraham that they would have a son, who would found nations.

The beliefs of Judaism are found not in an individual volume but in many sacred texts, traditions, and laws. An important figure among the early Jews was Moses, who lived about four hundred years after Abraham. Moses received the Ten Commandments from God. He led the Israelites out of slavery in Egypt and into the Promised Land. According to Jewish tradition, God had promised this land to descendants of Abraham.

Note that the term *Israelite* refers to the followers of Abraham in the ancient lands of the eastern Mediterranean. The term *Israeli* refers to a citizen of today's national of Israel, either Jew or Arab.

Corpses of Jews lie in the streets of a Ukrainian town, in the kind of pogroms that Golda's family fled from.

socialist state, where everyone owned the land and resources equally, and—they hoped—Jews would be treated as equals.

The Russian authorities could attack people who expressed either of these views at any time. Recognizing his family's continual fear, Moshe started gathering money to buy a boat ticket to the United States. He crossed the ocean and planned to send for the rest of the family as soon as he had enough money. With Moshe gone, the family lost the right to live outside the Pale, so they moved to Pinsk (now in Belarus), where Blume's parents lived.

Blume watched Sheyna become more involved with dangerous ideas. Through letters to Milwaukee, Wisconsin, where Moshe was now living, Blume urged her husband to get the family to America as quickly as possible. In 1906, Moshe sent the money for their passage. They had to leave secretly and sneak across the border into Poland, then take a train to the Belgian port city of Antwerp. Somehow they made it safely, and the family sailed to New York City. From there they took trains to Milwaukee, a growing city on the western shore of Lake Michigan.

Golda was eight when she moved to the United States. She carried two fears that would later play a role in her life—fear of pogroms and fear of hunger. She would fight the first fear by helping to build a nation for Jews in the eastern Mediterranean region called Palestine. She would fight the second fear by making farming one of the basic activities of Jews in Palestine.

CHAPTER TWO

Finding Her Voice

WHEN THE MABOVITCHES ARRIVED IN Milwaukee, Moshe, who now called himself Morris, immediately took them to a department store for new, American-looking clothing. Blume quickly realized that Morris, despite his apparent generosity, was not really earning a good living. Determined to help support her family, she hurried to open a small grocery store within the German Jewish community where they lived.

The Jews in Milwaukee existed in two different cultures. The German Jews, who had been there for many years, looked down on the Jews who had arrived more recently from Eastern Europe. The German Jews proudly spoke "true" German or English, while the newcomers spoke Yiddish, the type of German spoken in Jewish communities throughout Europe and North America. Sheyna, who had hoped for a wonderful new life in America, was ashamed to find herself in a narrow-minded community that seemed to be just like the one they had left.

Up to this time, Goldie's only schooling had consisted of learning to read and write with Sheyna's help, although her mother thought it was a bad idea—after all, Blume believed, education just distracted women from the home. But in Milwaukee, Goldie attended the Fourth Street School (its name was later changed to Golda Meir School) and avidly absorbed everything she was taught. Unlike Sheyna, she didn't let her surroundings depress her; she just ignored them whenever possible.

This typical shop in old Milwaukee, Wisconsin, is similar to the one Golda helped her mother run.

Golda's class at Fourth Street School in Milwaukee; she is the last person in the first row (circled).

From her earliest years in Milwaukee, Golda opened her mother's store in the mornings before school. Because of her work in the shop, Golda was frequently absent from school. Finally, a truant officer came by and told her mother that it was illegal for a child under fourteen not to attend school. Even after that encounter with the law, Goldie was still occasionally late to school. Despite her absences and her need to learn a second language, Golda graduated at the top of her junior high class. During the graduation ceremony, she gave a speech on the importance of being useful to society.

Goldie already had discovered the joys of public speaking, as well as being socially useful. At eleven, she helped organize her classmates to raise money for other classmates who needed books. She planned a public gathering at which she spoke about the financial problems new immigrants faced. Amazingly, she had been an immigrant herself just three years earlier.

Golda's sister, Sheyna, had trouble settling down, primarily because she was always fighting her parents' old-world ideas. She tried to move away from Milwaukee but could not earn a living and had to return home. Learning that an old boyfriend from Pinsk, Sharmai Korngold, had moved to New York, she located him and persuaded him to move to Milwaukee. Blume was not pleased, and when Korngold arrived, she forbade Sheyna to see him.

Sheyna developed a serious lung disease known as consumption, now called tuberculosis. She was sent to Denver, Colorado, to a Jewish hospital to recuperate, and Korngold followed her. After her recovery, the two married. They remained in Denver.

After finishing eighth grade, Golda prepared to move on to high school. But her old-fashioned mother saw no point in educating a girl. In fact, Blume feared an education would make Golda less attractive to a potential husband. Blume wanted Golda to quit school and get married. But Golda's dream was to become a teacher. She wanted to go to high school and then to a teacher's college.

ESCAPE TO DENVER

Golda managed to start high school in 1912, but Blume fought her every day. For Golda, the last straw came when her mother, hoping to get Golda married quickly, had a matchmaker bring young men to their home to meet her.

Determined not to have to keep fighting her mother, Golda collected her savings, borrowed money from friends, and even held English classes for immigrants at ten cents an hour so she could flee Milwaukee. Her best friend, Regina, helped her sneak out to the train station on a day when her parents thought she was on her way to school. She took a train to Denver, where she moved into the tiny apartment of her sister and Korngold. Golda had little contact with her parents for the next two years.

Golda attended high school in Denver, and on evenings and weekends she received a different kind of education—she joined Sheyna and Korngold when they hosted gatherings. Fascinating young people came to the Korngold apartment to sip tea and to debate such subjects as Zionism, women's suffrage, and the value of labor unions to protect workers' rights.

Golda listened and learned, and she began to focus her attention on Zionism, the belief that Jews should return to the Promised Land, or Abraham's Canaan. The Promised Land was thought to be Palestine, an area of the Middle East that was part of the Ottoman

Golda (*center* rear) was photographed at a picnic with her high school classmates.

Empire, an Arab empire controlled from Turkey. Golda especially liked the version of Zionism promoted by A. D. Gordon, a Russian who had immigrated to Palestine in 1904. He believed in Labor Zionism, which held that the future of Jews depended on their becoming farmers and laborers.

Golda often flirted with the young men who came around to debate. She soon realized that Sheyna was keeping just as stern an eye on her as her mother would have. After one major fight with her sister, Golda decided to leave Sheyna's household. Certain that she would not be welcome back in Milwaukee, she remained in Denver, where she rented a room and found a job in a department store.

Golda fought loneliness by accepting the invitations of Morris Meyerson, a quiet, self-educated music lover and part-time sign painter from Lithuania whom she had met at Sheyna's house. (Meyerson's sister had been a patient at the Jewish hospital when Sheyna was being treated for consumption there.) Golda came to admire Meyerson, who gave her gifts and wrote her poems. She wrote her friend Regina that he had a "beautiful soul."

Golda and Meyerson soon talked about the possibility of marriage, even though Meyerson had to support his own family. But another possibility opened up when Golda's father wrote to her for the first time in two years. He and Blume were giving in. If Golda would return to Milwaukee, she could finish high school and then go on to teacher's college.

YEARNING TOWARD ZION

Back in Milwaukee, Golda found her parents better off financially than when she had left, and her younger sister, now using the name Clara, had become a teenager. Golda quickly finished high school, and in October 1916 she began training to become a teacher at Milwaukee State Normal School (later, the University of Wisconsin-Milwaukee).

Much to Blume's dismay, Morris Meyerson wrote ardent love letters to Golda, several of which her mother steamed open. Golda and her mother had a screaming match, at the end of which Blume agreed not to invade her daughter's privacy again.

Each exchange of letters further indicated that Meyerson and Golda would have a future together, but Golda's hopes were actually directed elsewhere. She became sidetracked by the Great War (World War I) that was going on in Europe. She and her father began doing relief work to help Jews who had been displaced by the war. The Mabovitches frequently hosted lecturers who came to Milwaukee, and Golda became absorbed in discussions about the future of the Jews.

Increasingly, Golda spoke in public—even on street corners—about the plight of the Jews. One observer recorded that she was

 free of stage fright, courageous, possessing a reservoir of energy.

Zionist leaders began to take note of the enthusiastic young woman. They asked Golda to join them in Poale Zion (Workers of Zion), an organization aimed at preparing Jews for a life of work in Palestine. Golda was eager to join the Milwaukee Zionists, but she soon realized that they were more interested in helping the Jewish immigrants in their own city than taking action that would lead them to Palestine. And Golda was a person of action. She was captivated when Jews who had moved to Palestine came to Milwaukee to speak. She wanted to be one of those brave, dedicated people who lived on a kibbutz, which was an agricultural settlement "intent on making the desert produce food." It seemed unreasonable to her for a person to be a Zionist and not to make every effort to live in the Promised Land.

SKIRMISHES WITH MEYERSON

Growing in her determination to go to Palestine, Golda quit teacher's college so that she could earn money. She took a job at a local library to support her other activities. For example, when she learned about new pogroms taking place in Russia, she led a protest parade through downtown Milwaukee. Jews from many different organizations gathered at a meeting she led. National newspapers picked up the story of young Golda Mabovitch.

Meyerson disagreed with Golda's new focus. He thought she was exaggerating the bravery of Palestinian settlers, and he certainly didn't want to go there with her, as she was urging him to do. Criticizing the idealists and hoping to change her mind, he wrote, "Six weeks of struggle with the virgin soil will cure them of their 'idealism' permanently."

But Golda paid more attention to Zionism than she did to Meyerson. She talked to any small crowd that would listen to her on street corners. Her increasingly skillful speaking gradually brought her to the attention of a larger and larger circle. David Ben-Gurion, who later would be regarded as the founder of Israel, and Yitzhak Ben-Zvi, who would become Israel's second president, came to Milwaukee while recruiting soldiers for the Jewish Legion, a part of the British Army fighting the First World War.

Golda was scheduled to meet with Ben-Gurion, but Meyerson was in town. Hoping to meet with Ben-Gurion later, she chose to go to a concert with Meyerson. Ben-Gurion decided Golda was not serious enough about the Zionist cause, however, and he chose not to meet with her. Golda never again made the mistake of yielding to a private wish when she had a public duty. And she remained in awe of Ben-Gurion throughout most of the coming years.

From visitors to Milwaukee, Golda acquired an impression of the real Palestine, not just the Zionist dream she had held. She learned that conditions under the Ottomans were very bad, but she also developed a vision of what Palestine could be in the future. When Meyerson came to Milwaukee, she tried to share with him all that she had been doing and thinking, including her ideas about moving to Palestine. Morris told Golda what he had been reading and thinking, including his ideas about raising a family in the United States. Each barely realized that the other was speaking very differently about their future. Golda thought that she made herself clear—they would need to go to Palestine. And Meyerson thought he had made himself equally clear—they should remain in the United States.

Golda issued an ultimatum. If Meyerson didn't agree to go with her to Palestine, there would be no marriage. At first, Morris refused to give in, and Golda, in a huff, moved to Chicago, where she again worked in a library. But then the man who wanted only to live a quiet family life gave in to his tempestuous Golda.

In November 1917 the British issued what came to be called the Balfour Declaration. As the end of the Great War approached, the British expected to gain control of part of the vast region long controlled by the Ottoman Empire. This region included Palestine, the land at the eastern end of the Mediterranean Sea. British foreign secretary Lord Arthur Balfour wrote in a letter,

> **His Majesty's Government view with favour the establishment in Palestine of a national home for the Jewish people and will use their best endeavours to facilitate the achievement of this objective.**

Golda was elated. Perhaps this declaration would actually establish a true Jewish homeland in Palestine. Meyerson began to back off a bit from his firm stand against their departure. The two reached an agreement, and they were married at the Mabovitch home on December 24, 1917.

MOVING THEIR MARRIAGE

Although they were married, Golda and Morris Meyerson spent little time together. When Golda wasn't working, she was off conducting the business of Zionism. If she was at home, her Zionist friends were there, too, denying Morris the quiet he sought.

In 1918, Golda was excited to hear that the American Jewish Congress was being founded to encourage equal rights for Jews. The Zionists joined the organization in the hope that they could play a role in the settlements that would be established when the Great War ended. They wanted the Balfour Declaration to become reality. Many other Jews, however, rejected the idea of a nation for Jews. They were afraid that such a homeland would make them stand out even more than they already did.

LOOKING FAR AHEAD

Part of Palestine became Israel, a modern nation occupying a narrow strip of land on the eastern edge of the Mediterranean Sea. A land of hills and deserts, it is about the same size as New Jersey. The Dead Sea, located on Israel's border with Jordan, is the lowest spot on the Earth's surface.

Israel joins the other countries that make up the region called the Middle East. Those countries are Lebanon to the north; mostly Jordan to the east, with a small section of Syria at the northern end; and the Sinai Peninsula, which belongs to Egypt, to the southwest. Gaza, a small strip of land on the Mediterranean, adjoins Sinai. Gaza is the home of many Arab people usually referred to as Palestinians. Arabs who live in Israel are called Israeli Arabs.

The Israeli flag features the Star of David, symbol of Judaism.

Golda was chosen to represent Milwaukee at the first American Jewish Congress meeting in Philadelphia. She sat, enthralled, through the long debates and cast her own vote on the positions the group decided to take. She was thrilled to be able to vote because women could not yet vote in U.S. elections.

When Golda returned to Milwaukee, the national leadership of Poale Zion asked her to become a fund-raiser and speaker for the organization. Without even discussing with Morris the pros and cons of the position, she quit her job at the library and began to travel around the country. Each time Golda returned home, Morris welcomed her with flowers and hoped that this time she would stay. Instead, still reluctant, he found himself one of a party of seventeen pioneering Jews setting off for Palestine in 1921. What they found was nothing like the "land of milk and honey" that the recruiting brochures had promised.

CHAPTER THREE

The Land She Meant to Tame

G OLDA, MORRIS, GOLDA'S SISTER SHEYNA (who had impulsively left her husband), Golda's friend Regina, Regina's husband, and a small party of other "pioneers" sailed on the SS *Pocahontas* on May 23, 1921. Their ship to Palestine almost didn't reach its destination. The ship was in poor shape, ready for the scrap heap. The crew mutinied several times. There were fires on board, and someone murdered the chief engineer. Somehow the small group from Milwaukee reached land, but not in Palestine. Instead, they landed in Alexandria, Egypt, because the Arab boat owners in Jaffa's harbor refused to carry the Jews from the ship to land. From Alexandria, the settlers took a train to the dusty new town of Tel Aviv.

ERETZ YISRAEL

What was this land that Golda and Morris Meyerson were off to, willingly or not? The land became the nation of Israel, and the Meyersons' story is an integral part of that nation's story.

Exodus, the second book of the Bible, tells of God promising to deliver the Israelites out of slavery and to "a land flowing with milk and honey." Many Jews thought they would find such an economic promise in Palestine. Regardless of the reality of that promise, Jews felt that they were coming home.

Golda Mabovitch and her husband, Morris Meyerson

Ancient Israel is known to the Jews as Eretz Yisrael, meaning "Land of Israel." This is where Jews as a people were born. They claim the land based on stories of Israelite kingdoms in the Torah (the Five Books of Moses in the Bible). Those stories took place in the land called Palestine. References to Palestine abound in Jewish culture.

Many Jewish holidays commemorate events that took place in Palestine. For example, Sukkot, also called the Festival of Booths, is usually held in early October (according to the Jewish calendar, it starts on the fifteenth day of the month, called Tishrei). Rooted in the text of the book of Leviticus, Sukkot is a seven-day harvest festival that commemorates the dedication of Solomon's Temple. It is called the Festival of Booths because the Israelites went to Jerusalem for the dedication, and there they resided in booths, or sukkah. Some Jewish families build temporary outdoor structures, or booths, in which to eat their Sukkot feasts.

Solomon's Temple (actually, the *first* temple because it was destroyed and rebuilt several times) was completed and dedicated in the tenth century CE. In 586 BCE, however, the Babylonians conquered the Israelites, and most Jews moved to Babylonia. When Persia conquered Babylonia less than a hundred years later, the Persian king, Cyrus, allowed the Jews to return to Eretz Yisrael. They built the second Jewish Temple, and they remained there until they were defeated in an uprising against Rome in 135 CE.

Gradually the Jews' language, Hebrew, became Aramaic, which was the language of Babylon. It was in Aramaic that the Talmud was created. This document contains the history, customs, and laws of the Jews.

Some Jews remained in Eretz Yisrael, but they were ousted in 70 CE, when the Romans conquered the land. The Jews were forced to leave, and they spread throughout the Mediterranean world. The

Solomon's Temple in Jerusalem was destroyed by the Babylonians, who took the Jews into captivity.

movement of Jews away from the Land of Israel is called the Diaspora, meaning "scattering." Opening Palestine to Jews in the late nineteenth century would bring the Diaspora full circle.

RETURNING TO ZION

For many centuries, Jews believed that only God could take them back to Israel, through the actions of a messiah, or messenger. Then, in the nineteenth century, several rabbis wrote that it might be possible for humans to start the work of returning Jews to the Promised Land, or Zion. Not until about 1890 was the term *Zionism* used for this belief.

Jews around the world disagreed about how the return to Zion should happen. Followers of Labor Zionism—Golda's chosen philosophy—felt that working-class Jews should go to Palestine, work the soil, and gradually create their own country out of their labor. The alternative philosophy, founded by Theodor Herzl, can be called Political Zionism. Herzl felt that Jews should create their own state by persuading powerful nations to back the idea of a Jewish homeland. Labor Zionism gradually overshadowed Political Zionism.

When anti-Semitic pogroms began, Jews began to move out of Russia. Some went to the United States, but others, calling themselves Lovers of Zion, chose Palestine. The immigrations to Palestine that took place from 1881 to 1904 are referred to as the First Aliyah (meaning "progress" or "advance"). The goal of the immigrants was to establish small-scale settlements in Palestine.

These first immigrants went to Palestine to work the land. They never mentioned a dream of forming a Jewish nation. If they had, Jews in Western Europe would have ignored them. Western European Jews were afraid that their home countries would see them as unpatriotic if they supported a separate nation. However, in the twenty-five years of the First Aliyah, about 30,000 Jews moved from Europe to Palestine.

The newcomers were surprised to find that they were not the first Jews in Palestine. At least 25,000 Jews already lived there, mainly in four cities—Jerusalem, Hebron, Safed, and Tiberias. These Jews, most of whom were scholars, are now referred to as the Old Settlement. Jewish residents of Palestine as a whole are called the *Yishuv*, which means "settlement." People used this term until 1948, when the Yishuv became the State, or nation, of Israel.

THE FOUNDER OF ZIONISM

Theodor Herzl (1860–1904) was a secular Jew from Vienna, Austria. Working as a newspaperman, he watched the 1894 trial of Captain Alfred Dreyfus in Paris, France. A Jewish artillery officer, Dreyfus was accused of spying for Germany, found guilty of treason, and sent to Devil's Island, the French island prison off South America, for life. Authorities later identified the man who actually had committed the treasonable deed, but the French army refused to reconsider Dreyfus's case; they even created false documents that made the Jew appear guilty. The whole of France debated the Dreyfus case for many months. Ultimately, Dreyfus was exonerated and set free.

Herzl became disgusted with the French army's lies. He grew certain that Jews would never be absorbed into European society. In a book published in 1896, *Der Judenstaat* (*The Jewish State*), he argued that Jews should have their own country, not on religious grounds but on political grounds. He even asked the sultan of Turkey to grant Palestine to the Jews. The sultan refused.

Others had long been proposing a similar independent nation for Jews. The idea was called Zionism. *Zion* comes from the Hebrew word *Tzi-yon*, referring to the land occupied by the Israelites in ancient times, particularly Jerusalem. These proponents were called the Children of Zion.

The new and the old settlements did not get along very well. Many of the newcomers were not at all religious, a fact that people of the Old Settlement frowned upon. The Turks of the Ottoman Empire, which controlled the region, also disliked the newcomers, whom they saw as a political threat.

In 1901 the Jewish National Fund purchased the first Jewish-owned land that became part of the future nation of Israel. The international Zionist movement had created the fund. Jews all over the world had collected pennies to contribute to the purchase. The collection boxes were blue and white, which are the colors used in the Jewish *tallit*, or prayer shawl. Eventually blue and white became the colors of the Israeli flag. Over the following years, more Jews moved to Palestine in the Second Aliyah, but they were always vulnerable to attacks by Arabs who didn't like seeing Jews buying up more and more land. Like Golda Mabovitch, Jews the world over were excited when the British issued the Balfour Declaration in 1917.

THE BALFOUR DECLARATION

Many people believe that Lord Balfour declared a potential Jewish homeland in Palestine as a gift for Chaim Weizmann, a Russian chemist who had moved to England and had developed a process that was very useful in fighting the Great War: a way to make artificial acetone, which is used to manufacture ammunition. Lord Balfour asked Weizmann what he wanted in payment for his invention. Weizmann replied, simply, "A national home for my people." He later became the first president of Israel, the national home for his people.

That makes a nice story, but in reality, Lord Balfour made his declaration because the British wanted American and Russian Jews

Early Zionist settlers of the First Aliyah

to join their side during World War I. They also wanted to create a geographic buffer zone that would protect the Suez Canal from attacks by troops of the Ottoman Empire.

The Balfour Declaration actually appeared in a letter to Lord Rothschild, the head of the French branch of the powerful international Rothschild family. Lord Balfour didn't actually make any demands. He just said, "His Majesty's Government view with favour the establishment in Palestine of a national home for the Jewish people." Then he added that it was "clearly understood that nothing shall be done which may prejudice the civil and religious rights of existing non-Jewish communities in Palestine." This addition has caused trouble ever since.

DAVID BEN-GURION

The man who would later become known as the Founding Father of Israel was born David Grün in Plonsk, Poland, which was part of Russia, in 1886. His father was a lawyer and an avid Zionist. David was educated at home and at a Hebrew school. As he grew up, he spoke only Hebrew with his friends.

As a child, Grün caught his father's passion for a Jewish homeland. He knew that Zionism was not something just to be talked about. It required action by all those who believed that Jews should have a land of their own in Palestine. At age eighteen, he joined Poalei Tziyon ("Workers of Zion"). Within a year, he moved to Palestine, where he went to work picking oranges. He helped found the first agricultural workers' commune, the forerunnner of the kibbutz.

In 1912 young Grün went to Turkey to study law. While there he took on a Hebrew name (*ben* means "son of"), which he used proudly when he returned to Palestine. The Promised Land was completely under the control of the Ottoman Empire at the time, and during World War I, Ottoman officials ordered Ben-Gurion to leave because he was a national of an enemy country, Russia. He went to New York, where he met the woman who became his wife, Paula Monbaz. Ben-Gurion soon joined the Jewish Legion, a part of the British Army dedicated to taking Palestine out of Ottoman hands. However, the army refused to let the Jews fight in Palestine.

When the Balfour Declaration became public after the war,

Ben-Gurion knew immediately that the British would never voluntarily give up Palestine; the Jews would have to claim it. As he had said earlier, a homeland "is the historic creation and the collective enterprise of a people, the fruit of its labor, bodily, spiritual and moral, over a span of generations." Ben-Gurion then started to concentrate on what he saw as the three main things the Jews would need: new immigration into Palestine, the ability to defend themselves, and the arms necessary to do so. Basically a realist, he lived to achieve the dream, but he remained pragmatic.

In 1946 the Jewish Agency, an organization that helped Jews emigrate to Palestine, appointed Ben-Gurion to organize the Jewish defenses of Palestine. He had little time to complete the task before the British Mandate, a formal agreement made after the Great War giving Britain power to rule Palestine, expired. Ben-Gurion had to change the Jewish military from guerrilla fighters to a modern army. The Jews were ready to fight when the United Nations (UN) declared Israel a nation, and the Arabs moved in from surrounding lands to try to destroy it.

Ben-Gurion served as prime minister of Israel several times during the coming years. He retired fully in 1970.

Golda Meyerson regarded it as a privilege to work side by side with Ben-Gurion. She saw him as "the very personification of Israel throughout the world. . . . he was the only one of whom it could be said that he was literally indispensable to the Jewish people in its struggle for independence."

Palestine was not an empty land waiting for the Jews to return. It was occupied by thousands of Arabs, who had borne the rule of the Ottoman Empire for centuries. When the Balfour plan became public, rioting broke out in Jerusalem. Arab fighters attacked the Jewish community. They killed several and wounded hundreds.

When the First World War ended, the victors met and decided who would control the land of the Ottoman Empire, which had sided with the German losers. The League of Nations (forerunner of the UN) gave control of Syria to France. Great Britain was given the order—eventually called the British Mandate—to oversee an oddly shaped territory lying between Syria, Iraq, Arabia, and Egypt. Later, the area east of the Jordan River became the nation of Jordan. The area to the west, down to the Gulf of Aqaba, became Palestine.

When the British Mandate was issued in 1920, there were perhaps 85,000 Jews in a Palestinian population of about 750,000. The number of Jews increased greatly after the Third Aliyah—of which Golda and the reluctant Morris were part—started in 1919.

Beginning in 1921, the British government issued a series of White Papers (so called because of their white covers) on its plans for the British Mandate. The government issued most White Papers in response to Arab riots against the Jews. Each paper grew progressively less focused on helping Jews settle in a homeland and more concerned with keeping the Arabs in Palestine happy. The Arabs of the region inhabited much of the route to India and controlled considerable oil resources. As the British issued statement after statement, the Jews in Palestine went from jubilant to discouraged. They gradually came to accept that they would have

THE HEBREW LANGUAGE

Ancient Hebrew, the language of the Israelites, was rarely spoken, but it was never forgotten in four thousand years because it was the language of the Torah. Eliezer Ben-Yehuda, a Russian-born Jew who moved to Palestine in 1881, began to develop Hebrew into a modern spoken language. Until then, the only language that Jews around the world generally had in common was Yiddish, which means "Jewish." Yiddish is a dialect of German that people have spoken since probably the tenth century. Before Golda Meyerson went to Israel, the only Hebrew she knew was the little she had learned by going briefly to Talmud School as a child. Golda's family spoke Yiddish. Today, no matter where Jewish immigrants to Israel come from, they are required to start studying Hebrew as soon as possible.

to form their country by themselves, since they apparently could not count on the British to help them.

LIFE ON A KIBBUTZ

Golda intended to take up life right away on a kibbutz (plural: kibbutzim), which means "gathering." A kibbutz was the basic form of communal life in Palestine after the secular Jews started moving there. In effect, they replaced the earlier life of religious study with a life of physical labor. A kibbutz was usually a farm, developed on land that had long been regarded as hopeless. The members would plant trees, cultivate the land, and drain swamps. They were often able to buy the land because it was marshy and, consequently, infested with the mosquitoes that carried malaria.

Upon their arrival in Palestine, Golda and Morris went to Kibbutz Merhavia, one of about twenty-five kibbutzim in existence at the time. Located on the Plain of Jezreel, it still exists today.

People became new members of a kibbutz via a vote of the established members. Kibbutz Merhavia rejected Golda and Morris twice. The reason was immediately clear. Most of the members were single men, and they wanted more single women to join them! In addition, the women on the kibbutz thought that an American woman would be too soft to do the hard work necessary. After all, up to that time, about one-third of the American women who had come to Palestine had gone back home.

When the Meyersons bravely applied a third time, Kibbutz Merhavia granted them a one-month probationary period to prove that they were indeed willing to work hard.

Golda was committed to the idea that the Jews who worked the land were earning a country of their own. If someone else did the work, the Jews did not deserve a country. She promptly demonstrated that women and men deserved equal rights. Golda climbed a high ladder on a water tower to remove a clog to the water supply. Such a clog was a common occurrence, but the kibbutz women had always waited for a man to do the repair.

Merhavia was not a beautiful place—certainly not a "land of milk and honey"—when the Meyersons arrived in September 1921. Located in a swamp, it consisted of only a few trees and a few huts, surrounded by a cement wall with holes through which the kibbutzniks (kibbutz members) could shoot if Arabs from nearby villages attacked. Their work was to drain the swamp and to plant vegetables and trees. Donations from the Jewish National Fund paid for their living expenses. Sales of milk from their small dairy farm provided a little bit of extra cash.

The kibbutzniks lived communally. They slept in barracks (except for a few private rooms for couples) and ate together. Each member did the work assigned to him or her. Golda's first tasks were to pick almonds and to dig holes in the rocky soil to plant tree seedlings. Her hands bled, her back ached, and she was vulnerable to the debilitating (and sometimes fatal), insect-borne disease of malaria. Toilets were just holes in the ground. Members washed clothing for the whole group, and whoever needed fresh clothes received whatever was handy. There was no such thing as private ownership. Because freshwater had to be carried by donkey from half an hour away, members never wasted the water on such luxuries as baths.

But Golda was where she wanted to be, and she never once thought about giving up. She rejoiced in living an ideal that she had dreamed about for years. When the kibbutzniks were not working, they planned their work and talked about every subject imaginable. She found this life completely fulfilling.

Although most kibbutzniks were not religious, Friday nights, which begin the Jewish Sabbath, were special. Golda often decorated the dining table, to the jeering of others who saw no reason to fancy things up. She also gradually improved the food.

Morris was neither happy nor completely unhappy. He liked the scenery around Merhavia and found some satisfaction in the physical labor. However, he hated the lack of privacy and the fact that no one else loved music as much as he did. He also disliked the fact that he saw even less of Golda than he had in the United States. Golda wasn't paying much attention to the state of her marriage. She wanted to have children, but Morris refused to do so on the kibbutz, where children

Women kibbutzniks worked in the fields alongside the men, often accompanied by their children.

were raised together in a separate building and parents could visit them only occasionally.

Golda was the only person at Merhavia who cared about the organization of the Yishuv as a whole. The kibbutzniks chose her to represent them at the first convention of kibbutzim, held at Degania. It was there that the Jewish leaders, including David Ben-Gurion, learned that they had among them an attractive young woman who knew English and was a skilled public speaker. They questioned Golda in great detail and learned that she was a true Zionist. They assigned her work that would benefit the whole Yishuv.

Golda's first duty was to accompany the wife of a British Labor Party leader around Palestine. For this journey, she had to beg the kibbutzniks at Merhavia to let her buy a new dress. Her persistence earned her a first broad view of the land the Jews hoped to call their own.

Morris became seriously ill with malaria and was in danger of dying from the high fevers. Golda decided to give up her beloved kibbutz life and take him to Tel Aviv, a new city of about 30,000 people, where he could be treated. She felt that her life at the heart of Labor Zionism was probably over.

CHAPTER FOUR

Working Her Way Up

A S MORRIS WAS RECOVERING IN TEL AVIV, an old friend met with Golda and asked if the couple would move to Jerusalem so Golda could take a job in the Yishuv's public works office. They accepted, and it was in that ancient city that Golda gave birth to her son, Menachem (meaning "comfort"), in 1924, and her daughter, Sarah, in 1926. Menachem and Sarah were Sabras. This term for native-born Israelis comes from the fruit of the prickly pear cactus, which is tough and thorny on the outside and soft on the inside. The term was first used in 1931.

Golda's parents left the United States and followed her to Palestine when Menachem was born. They settled in the new town of Herzlia, named after Theodor Herzl, the primary founder of Zionism. Blume opened a restaurant, one of the few in Palestine. Golda's father, still a carpenter, built their home with his own hands.

The Meyersons led lives of poverty in Jerusalem. The only home they could afford to rent on Golda's tiny salary was at the end of a dusty road. They had no indoor plumbing, gas, or electricity. In order to pay for Menachem's nursery school, Golda washed the school's laundry. She found urban poverty harder to accept than the poverty of life on the kibbutz, primarily because the kibbutzniks were part of a dynamic group with goals and sociability. Her urban neighbors, on the other hand, were traditional Orthodox Jews with no sympathy for her work toward building a Jewish nation.

By 1925, the Jews in Palestine had built the Hebrew University in Jerusalem.

Only briefly after her babies were born did Golda hold a job that involved women in a traditional way. In 1928, she became secretary of the Women's Labor Council. The position involved a lot of travel, and she had to move to Tel Aviv. Morris did not want to go, but Golda went anyway, and she took the children with her. Her move marked a distinct break in their marriage. She and Morris would never really live together again, but they did not get divorced until 1945. Golda later wrote about Morris,

> **He had always been quiet and reserved. To the outside world he may have appeared ineffectual or unsuccessful; but the truth is that his inner life was very rich—richer than mine, for all my activity and drive—and he shared it generously with his close friends, his family and, particularly, his children.**

Golda's new job entailed getting vocational training for the many young women who had romantic dreams of Labor Zionism on farms (rather like Golda herself had had) but no farming experience. Golda had little real interest in the job but was determined to succeed at whatever work was asked of her.

JERUSALEM

For hundreds of years, the Israelites of ancient times were split into many different clans. About 2,500 years ago, King David united the tribes under his rule and made Jerusalem the capital of his kingdom. Solomon, David's son, built his first temple there. The city remained under Jewish control for six hundred years. Since then, it has fallen into many different hands, some Jewish, some Roman, and finally Christian and Arab. Romans executed a Jew named Jesus in Jerusalem. Today, it is a holy city for three religions—Judaism, Christianity, and Islam. Control of the city is an important sticking point preventing peace between Israel and Palestine.

Scientist Albert Einstein and several other world-famous Jews, such as Sigmund Freud, founded Hebrew University of Jerusalem. Einstein and Freud were its governors when it opened for classes in 1925.

Rooftops in Jerusalem representing the three faiths of the holy city

Labor Zionists believed that settlers could achieve a Jewish homeland only by hard work.

During the early days of the Yishuv, there were two labor-oriented political parties that qualified as socialist. One was the Marxist Poelei Tsion, and the other was the non-Marxist Hapoel Hatzair, or Young Worker Party. Although socialism has many flavors, the basic belief is that the people as a whole, not individuals, should control the

means of production and ownership of land. Even in the few years before Golda went to Palestine, the socialist basis of the Yishuv had declined. Throughout her life, however, she remained committed to socialist beliefs and belonged to labor-oriented political parties. The names of the parties to which she belonged changed several times over the years. The most consistent name was Mapai, which was an acronym for the Hebrew words meaning "Labor Party of the Land of Israel."

Golda was continually torn between her desperate desire to do well at her job and her desire to be a firm, loving, hands-on mother to her two children. Usually her work won out, and she often had to leave Menachem and Sarah in the care of others while she traveled, both in Palestine and abroad. Sometimes Morris would come from Jerusalem to care for the children.

THE TRAVELER

Golda's first trip back to the United States took place in 1929. Pioneer Women, a Labor Zionist woman's organization based in the United States, sponsored her. Golda's Labor Zionism was not very popular in the United States, however, so it was a struggle to get Jewish groups to listen to her. The groups that did listen were made up of European immigrants who often spoke Yiddish at home. They heard about the nitty-gritty of life on a kibbutz, not beautiful phrases about the ambitions of the Jewish people.

Golda felt like a fish out of water in the United States, as the country had changed greatly since she left. Clearly, this was no longer her nation. She took time to visit her sister Clara, who was married and living in Cleveland, Ohio. The two sisters had little in common now.

Golda returned home to find that Arabs in neighboring areas had increased their attacks on Jewish villages and even on Jerusalem itself. She tried to enlist in the Haganah, the Jewish defense organization, but they saw no use for her.

The following year, she went to England for the Conference of Socialist Women, at which she was pleased to learn that women around the world were interested in Palestine and the life there. She went to England at other times, too, in an attempt to understand the British government's increasing willingness to placate the Arabs in Palestine.

In 1932, Golda's six-year-old daughter, Sarah, became very ill, and the treatment she received was doing her no good. Golda worried that her little daughter would just waste away. She decided to take Sarah to the United States for diagnosis and treatment. Conveniently, the Executive Council had work for her to do in the United States at the same time. Both doctors and family members thought Golda was crazy to take a terribly ill child across an ocean by ship, but she felt she had no choice.

The journey lasted two weeks, but Sarah survived to reach Beth Israel Hospital in New York City. Doctors diagnosed her with a kidney disease that could be treated easily, and she was soon in perfect health.

A greatly relieved Golda set off on a new round of visits with the Pioneer Women. She was determined to build the deteriorating Labor Zionism movement in the United States. For many weeks she spoke to people, tried to raise funds, and looked for new enthusiasts who would move to Palestine. She also wrote articles for the magazine that the Pioneer Women published. She became so popular that Goldie Meyerson Clubs formed throughout the country.

Many American Jews had a rather romantic view of life in Palestine. One Pioneer Women official, Rebekah Kohut, wrote,

> Those who have visited Palestine in the past few years speak with the utmost admiration of the *haluzah* [female Zionist pioneer], who with face uplifted toward the Eastern sun, her shoulders straightened by the new freedom, with her hands eagerly mothers the neglected soil which she loves so dearly.

Golda scoffed at such romantics—but she still accepted their money.

Finally, after almost two years in the United States, Golda and her children returned to Palestine. The children had learned to speak English, but they hadn't learned how to keep their mother nearby. That situation was not about to change. On her return to Palestine, Golda Meyerson was asked to join the Yishuv Executive Committee. From that time on, she was always involved in governmental affairs on an equal basis with men.

Golda was frequently away from home. Menachem and Sarah were unhappy when she left, and in later years, Golda wondered if they ever forgave her for not being there when they got home from school, or for being away so much of the time. Golda's sister, Sheyna, tried to persuade Golda to be a better mother.

GOVERNMENT OR UNION?

Golda Meyerson devoted most of her adult life to the Histadrut (United Federation of Labor). The founders of the Histadrut stated, "It is the aim of the United Federation of all the workers and laborers of Palestine who live by the sweat of their brows without exploiting the toil of others, to promote land settlement, to involve itself in all economic and cultural issues affecting labor in Palestine, and to build a Jewish workers' society there."

The organization built its own factories, housing developments, health care system, and newspapers. Eventually it became the largest employer in Palestine. In 1959, Israeli Arabs were given membership in the Histadrut.

Golda always felt guilty about her absences, but she also continued to feel that the Palestinian Jews needed the best she could give. Palestine always won.

THE HISTADRUT

In 1920, David Ben-Gurion founded the Histadrut (United Federation of Labor). It became the umbrella organization for many labor unions, but it also ran a bank, owned various chains of stores, and even owned a bus line. In the early years, the Histadrut ran virtually everything in the Yishuv, which made Ben-Gurion the leader of the Jewish Community of Palestine. Later he would become the nation's first prime minister.

When Golda was invited to serve on the Histadrut Executive Council, she became the only woman who worked with the men who ran Palestine and then Israel. Many found her very attractive and flirted with her. Since she had left her husband, she usually felt able to respond. In her autobiography Golda never wrote about her romances with the men who were forming Israel. But in the preface of his 1988 book *Golda: The Romantic Years*, Ralph G. Martin writes,

> That was the single great surprise for me in this book—Golda's beauty as a young woman. That full firm figure, the long lustrous hair, the magnetic sparkle, the way she threw her head back when she laughed. One could quickly understand why so many men chased her and wanted her.

CHAPTER FIVE

Making A Nation

B EFORE THE JEWS IN PALESTINE FORMED THEIR own nation, their efforts were completely entangled with what was going on in the wider world. It wasn't just the neighboring Arabs they had to deal with. It was also the Germans who were determined to destroy all Jews. The British were determined to placate the Arabs, while the Americans wanted to appear sympathetic but did little to encourage Jews to come to the United States. Finally, all the players became involved in World War II.

In the midst of it all, Golda Meyerson played an ever-increasing role in what would become the birth of Israel.

Golda wrote in her autobiography about the jobs she held: "None of these, as I look back, were either easy to carry out or likely to make me particularly popular inside the Histadrut itself. But they did have one great asset. They all had to do with what in fact most concerned and interested me—the translation of socialist principles into the down-to-earth terminology of everyday life."

Golda's first task was one she hated: promoting the growth of tourism in Palestine. But as the low person on the totem pole, she did what she had to and was, at least, in the inner circle. She expanded her view of tourism to include sending Palestinian Jews to other countries to help new immigrants prepare for life in Palestine. She also took charge of the many orphaned children who somehow arrived in Palestine without adult support.

Whenever possible, Jewish children were rescued from German-occupied countries and taken to Palestine.

FIGHTING FOR EQUALITY

Because Golda cemented her belief in socialism, she often faced major battles within the Histadrut. She was determined to win these battles so that the equality of the members of the Yishuv would be true, both in the city and on the kibbutzim. She believed that everyone should share the burdens of life in their growing community. Regardless of what position a person held in the Yishuv, he or she was paid the same wage, varying only by the number of family members the worker had to support. Golda often had to fight other members of the executive council, especially David Ben-Gurion himself, to keep this practice going. Economic equality was especially important during the 1930s, when the Great Depression affected people all over the world. Golda herself earned no more than the woman who cleaned the Histadrut offices around her when she worked late at night.

One of Golda's biggest fights was to institute a regular tax to be paid by everyone who was working, even if they had very low-paying jobs. The Yishuv would use the revenue to support people without jobs. Despite rigorous arguments against the idea, Golda managed to establish an unemployment fund called Mifdeh, or "redemption." She was proud that, over the years, this fund provided support for thousands of families.

Golda's own popularity with the public was always in danger of collapsing. That didn't matter, however, because she wasn't in an elected position. The executive council knew exactly how valuable she was. They also knew that she remembered when someone opposed her and was capable of getting even.

DEFENDING THEMSELVES

At no time through these years were Jewish communities free from danger of attack by Arabs. These attacks ranged from something as simple but demoralizing as destroying thousands of trees planted by the kibbutzniks to derailing trains. Snipers continually shot at travelers on the road between Tel Aviv and Jerusalem, a road that Golda, as a member of the executive council, had to travel regularly. Their aim was to shut the road, thus starving the Jewish residents of Jerusalem.

The British prevented the Jews from having weapons but did nothing to stop Arab attacks until 1937. But what were the Jews to do?

In 1920, the Jews had formed an underground defense force called the Haganah. It functioned until Israel gained statehood. For the most part, the individual units of the Haganah were not organized into a widespread army. Instead, groups of farmers worked together to guarantee the safety of their families. Then, in 1929, a week of riots took place in the wake of a dispute over Jewish worship at the Western Wall (the remaining wall of Solomon's Temple) in Jerusalem. More than a hundred Jews and a hundred Arabs were killed in the fighting. As a result, the Haganah organized itself into a full-fledged army, involving most of the men and older boys in Jewish Palestine.

The Haganah still was not able to function as a real army. If the defense force had retaliated against the Arabs, the British would have cracked down on them. The British always had one major lever for keeping the Jews under control: they could limit the immigration of Jews into Palestine. Since the Jews did not want this to happen, they could only protect themselves; they could not carry the battle into Arab neighborhoods. One of Golda's tasks was to find public support for a tax that would pay to keep the Haganah active.

The leaders of the Haganah defense force did not believe in retaliation or acts of terrorism. Young men who did not agree with this approach formed two other military organizations that had no qualms about fighting in any way possible to get the British out of Palestine.

Woman as well as men trained to serve in the Haganah, the Jewish defense force in Palestine.

These were the Irgun and the Lehi, also called the Stern Gang. At various times, both groups were regarded as terrorist groups. The Haganah, on the other hand, later served as the basis of the Israeli Army.

A NEW HOPE

In 1936, the Grand Mufti of Jerusalem—the Muslim leader in the Middle East—called for a general strike in Palestine. All Arabs were to refrain from doing their work. The mufti hoped that this would halt all activity in the Yishuv and that further immigration of Jews would be outlawed. Instead, the Jews just doubled their efforts and did all the work that Arabs ordinarily would have done. When the Arabs closed the port at Jaffa, the Jews opened a new port at Tel Aviv, and shipping continued. Golda Meyerson even became involved in trying to buy ships in London.

The Arab strike was called off so that the British Peel Commission could decide what to do about the problem. The members of the commission traveled throughout Palestine to see what they could learn. Golda was responsible for showing them around and answering their questions.

The Arabs hoped that the commission would stop all immigration of Jews. Instead, the commission recommended that Palestine be partitioned into an Arab state and a Jewish state, with Jerusalem as an international zone. To Golda's dismay, the other leaders of the Histadrut accepted the plan, despite the fact that the amount of land granted as the Jewish state was terribly small. But she need not have worried, because the Arabs rejected the idea. Golda wrote in her autobiography, "The guiding principle behind the attitude of the Arabs . . . was exactly what it has been ever since: Decisions are made not on the basis of what is good for them, but on the basis of what is bad for us."

IMMIGRATION

There was no safety in Europe, either. The Nazis' policy of anti-Semitism had made that clear. Within months of taking office as chancellor of Germany in 1933, Adolf Hitler had dismissed all Jews from government office and had begun eliminating Jews from all businesses in Germany. Immediately, Jews began fleeing Germany, but there were few places that would welcome them.

Golda attended the International Conference on Refugees, held to discuss ways to deal with Jewish refugees, as an observer, "not even seated with the delegates, although the refugees under discussion were my own people," she wrote. However, as one of the few Jews who could speak English, she was often responsible for negotiations with the British.

The British refused to allow additional immigrants into Palestine. No nation, not even the United States, said they would take in Jewish refugees. Their excuse was the fact that unemployment was still high after the years of the Great Depression. Leaders could not see the statistics as human beings. Golda despaired. She was appalled that the world seemed willing to let the Jews die.

While Golda was in Europe, she negotiated about immigration during the day, but at night she was part of a group that was trying to find ships to carry Jews secretly from Europe to Palestine. That group called itself Mossad (short for the full Hebrew name meaning "Institute for Intelligence and Special Tasks"). Years later, Mossad became Israel's intelligence agency.

On her return to Palestine, Golda often looked through the window of her Tel Aviv apartment to spot ships slipping in past the British blockade at night. She would dash to the beach to help welcome the escapees to Palestine.

Sadly, the refugees weren't going to find safety in Palestine. The Arabs were still serious about eliminating Jews from the British Mandate. In 1939, the British backpedaled on establishing separate countries for Jews and Arabs. They announced that there was no way that partition could work. The British government issued a final White Paper, called the Malcolm MacDonald in honor of the prime minister. It called for the creation of a Palestinian state, with Arabs controlling the government. During the next five years, a total of only 75,000 Jews could enter Palestine. After that, there would be no more immigration. Again, Golda despaired.

WHY DIDN'T THE JEWS IMMIGRATE TO THE UNITED STATES?

By 1920, there were almost 4 million Jews in the United States, and most of them were immigrants. Starting in 1921, however, the U.S. Congress passed several laws restricting immigration. The nation's policy of holding its door open to anyone who wanted to enter was at an end. The restrictions applied mostly to southern and eastern Europeans, including Jews. The most famous Jew who did make it into the United States was scientist Albert Einstein, who entered in 1932. He became a U.S. citizen in 1940.

In 1938, when the world was finally recognizing that Nazis were deliberately targeting Jews, an international conference, promoted by U.S. president Franklin D. Roosevelt, was held in Évian-les-Bains, France. Nations met at the International Conference on Refugees to discuss Jewish refugees and what to do about them. By then, many other European countries had already begun limiting the number of Jews who could enter the country. So, too, had Australia, Canada, and other nations that had seemed to be potential safe havens. And the United States still limited the number of immigrants from Germany to fewer than 26,000 each year, a quota that was never filled.

At the end of the conference, prominent Jewish leader Chaim Weizmann said, "The world seemed to be divided into two parts—those places where the Jews could not live and those where they could not enter."

CHAPTER SIX

World War II and the United Nations

I n 1939, the British government of Neville Chamberlain gave in to Arab demands and decreed that there could be no more Jewish immigration into Palestine. The British issued a final White Paper that called for the creation of a Palestinian nation within a decade, with Jews as a minority. Jews could no longer purchase land in Palestine. The Grand Mufti calmly said that the 400,000 Jews already in Palestine would simply have to be expelled.

The Palestinian Jews were aghast. They knew that the Nazis in Germany were working to destroy Europe's Jews. They were certain that worse would come, and the only refuge Jews had was Palestine.

Up to that time, the dream of turning the Jewish presence in Palestine into a nation had been a distant one—few people were actively working toward such an idea. But then they realized that the British government was doing everything it could to prevent Jews who were just trying to survive from entering Palestine. The only way to fight for their homeland was to become independent. The British, whom the Jews realized were heroically fighting Hitler's evil forces, were also unwilling to help Jews survive against that evil. There were rumors that Germans were gassing Jews and even using the fat in Jews' bodies to make soap. The Jews believed the rumors, but the British scoffed. Even as war broke out with Germany's invasion of Poland in September 1939, Britain was reinforcing its blockade that kept Jews from entering Palestine.

Golda Meyerson at her desk in the Histadrut, early in World War II

The Jews knew that they would have to fight more than just the Arabs; from now on, they would also be fighting the British in Palestine. The Yishuv executive council formally authorized the Haganah as the Jewish army and began to search for ways to obtain weapons. Many people found these events disturbing—after all, Jews had always been a peaceful people. What did they know about fighting? But Golda asked, "What alternative do we have?"

The Jews were pulled in two different directions. As inhabitants of the British Mandate, they wanted to fight *with* the British Army against Germany. But at the same time, they were fighting *against* the British to try to rescue as many European Jews as they could. As David Ben-Gurion expressed it,

> **We shall fight the war as if there were no White Paper, and fight the White Paper as if there were no war.**

Golda joined the rest of the executive council in encouraging Palestinian Jews to join the British Army. After all, they would be helping Jews in Germany, and they would come home as experienced fighters. However, the British Army would accept a Jew in its ranks only if there was also an Arab volunteer to balance him. And the Arabs weren't signing up.

In January 1942, Hitler issued an official policy that the Germans called the Final Solution: the extermination of all Jews. Before the Allies defeated the Nazis in 1945, seven death camps had accounted for the murder of approximately 6 million Jews. The Jews call this geno-cide the Holocaust, meaning "the complete burning," or the *Shoah,* Hebrew for "calamity." In addition, another 5 or 6 million Gypsies (Rom), disabled people, communists, prisoners of war, homosexu-als, and religious dissidents were killed.

In spring of the same year, a group of Zionist leaders met in New York City. For the first time, Ben-Gurion urged that they work toward an actual nation for the Jews, instead of just a vague "homeland" within Palestine.

Although it was not widely known throughout the world, news of the Final Solution leaked out of Germany to Palestine. Jews had been persecuted throughout history, so they were familiar with the idea, but they still had a hard time believing the terrible stories they were hearing.

❝ There is no Zionism save the rescue of the Jews, ❞

Golda said. She and her colleagues on the executive council quickly learned that if they were to rescue European Jews, they would have to come up with huge amounts of money to secretly pay the people who could, they hoped, get the Jews out of Germany.

Golda was the executive council's favorite weapon because she was such a persuasive speaker. Once again, she set out to try to raise money. Her mission was hampered by the need to confess to would-be donors that it was unlikely that even a small percentage of the money raised would in any way affect the fate of Jews in Europe.

At one point, the executive council tried to get Britain to allow a brigade of Jewish fighters to be formed and sent to Europe. The British Army refused the offer. They knew that the Jewish fighters would have their own agenda. And they did—the Jewish fighters were intended to hunt for pockets of Jewish resistance, to reach survivors, and perhaps to bring them to safety.

During the war, Golda faced some personal problems. She had almost perpetual migraine headaches, but she refused to let them affect her long days and nights of work. Then, in 1943, her daughter, Sarah, quit high school to move onto one of the new kibbutzim located in the Negev Desert. The British had always declared the desert uninhabitable. But an important part of the Yishuv's long-range plans was to irrigate large parts of the Negev and turn them into agricultural communities supporting many thousands of immigrants. Golda visited her daughter at Kibbutz Revivim and was horrified when she saw how truly barren the location was.

NO CHANGE

On May 7, 1945, the war in Europe ended. Suddenly the Jews of Palestine had not a new task, but an old one that was even more formidable. They had to find a way to bring to Palestine the more than 600,000 Jews who were, somehow, still alive in concentration camps. Golda and her colleagues thought that surely the British would now relent in their opposition to immigration. Instead, the British gave up even the slightest pretense of someday allowing the Jews to have their own piece of Palestine. British troops helped prevent Jewish survivors from leaving the displaced-person camps in Europe and going to Palestine. U.S. president Harry Truman asked the British to allow 100,000 Jews to immigrate to Palestine, but the British government refused.

Jewish children imprisoned at Auschwitz, one of the Nazi concentration camps

The British prevented ships carrying immigrants from sailing to Palestine. When the British government persuaded the Italian government to stop two ships from sailing, the Jews refused to get off the ships. With the world watching, they declared a hunger strike. Golda organized and joined a sympathy hunger strike to take place in Jerusalem in the offices of the Jewish National Council. Because Jewish law required Jews to eat something for the Seder meal, the people in the offices gathered to swallow just one tiny bit of unleavened bread. Other than that one bite, they ate nothing.

After several days, international reaction forced the British to allow the ships to sail for Palestine. But other ships were taken under British control. The would-be immigrants once again found themselves imprisoned in camps, this time on the Mediterranean island of Cyprus.

IN CHARGE

June 29, 1946, came to be known as Black Saturday. British soldiers swarmed throughout Palestine. They arrested thousands of Jewish leaders, destroyed kibbutzim, and searched for Haganah weapons. The Jews had been tipped off, however, and the Haganah was able to hide its equipment.

Somehow, Golda Meyerson was not arrested. With the other executive council leaders in prison, she became acting head of the political department. She was, in effect, president of the Yishuv. She held this position until nationhood was proclaimed in 1948—even after Moshe Sharett, her predecessor, was released from prison. In later years, Golda was sad that she hadn't been sent to a detention camp like the other Yishuv leaders. She suggested that perhaps the camp could not have handled a woman prisoner. However, other women had been imprisoned, so she never knew why she had been left free.

Not everyone agreed that Golda was the person to run the Jewish settlements in Palestine. Many people thought she was too sweet and gentle. Others called her the only "man" on the executive council. Some Jews, especially the leaders of the Palmach, the military force of the Haganah, decided to ignore her.

Golda was decidedly becoming a "hawk," advocating an all-out war against the British. However, she was still hoping to negotiate the opening of Palestine to immigration. The British officers meeting with Golda were often astonished to see her acting as if she represented a sovereign nation instead of a group of people who happened to be living in the British Mandate.

At one time Golda went to see the British secretary of the Mandatory Government. She pointed out to him how terribly the Nazis had persecuted the Jews, and she said that those who survived now deserved to find peace in Palestine. He replied,

❝ Mrs. Meyerson, you must agree that if the Nazis persecuted the Jews, they must have had some reason for it. ❞

She walked out, saying only,

❝ That's what all the anti-Semites say. ❞

The continued arguments wore Golda down. Then, without warning, but under heavy pressure from attacks by the Urgun and the Haganah, the British government decided that it had had enough— after more than twenty-five years, it was time to end the British Mandate. They asked the newly formed UN to find a solution to the problem of Palestine.

A special committee of the UN arrived in Palestine in June 1947. The members wanted to see the situation for themselves. Golda Meyerson, working with the committee, was astonished to find that she needed to give them the history of Zionism and of Palestine. They had been sent to recommend a solution to a problem about which they knew nothing.

The committee witnessed a terrible demonstration of the relationship between Britain and the Jews when the British illegally boarded a Haganah ship called the *Exodus* and took it into Haifa harbor. The *Exodus* carried 4,500 survivors of the Holocaust. As Golda described,

> **If I live to be a hundred, I shall never erase from my mind the gruesome picture of hundreds of British soldiers in full combat dress, bearing and using clubs, pistols and grenades against the wretched refugees on the *Exodus*, 400 of whom were pregnant women determined to give birth to their babies in Palestine.**

British troops forcing Jews off a ship in Germany to prevent them
from immigrating to Palestine

Golda and other Palestinian Jews were appalled when they
learned that the survivors were to be caged and shipped back to Germany, the land of their horrors and degradation.

The UN committee did nothing to stop the British action, but its
members quickly voted to recommend to the UN General Assembly
that Palestine be partitioned into a Jewish state and an Arab state. In
addition, they proposed that Jerusalem and its immediate surroundings be made an international city.

The Arabs, still determined that the Jews never be given a homeland in Palestine, threatened war once again. The British insisted that partition should take place only if both Jews and Arabs supported the idea, which wasn't going to happen. Golda and all of Palestine knew that if the UN decided to give a permanent nation to the Jews, a ferocious war would break out.

Golda made several secret trips to Europe and the United States, primarily to raise funds. Her most memorable secret mission was to meet with King Abdullah, the ruler of Jordan, in November 1947. Originally part of the British Mandate as Transjordan, that country had become the Hashemite Kingdom of Jordan (Hashem is the name of the royal family) in 1946. The king was willing to talk with the Jews because the leader of the Arabs in Palestine, the Grand Mufti of Jerusalem, was his sworn enemy. King Abdullah did not want to see another Arab state in the area because he would lose land and clout. He promised Golda that he would not fight against the Jews.

Just before the UN vote that released the dogs of war, the Jews in Palestine received word that King Abdullah was going to change his mind. Golda secretly contacted him and reminded him of his promise. He said he would keep his promise, as a Bedouin, a king, and a man who would never break a promise given to a woman. Golda, dressed in Arab clothing, made a secret visit to Abdullah in Amman. The king proposed that the Jews wait for a Jewish nation of Israel to be formed, but Golda refused. If necessary, she said, let there be war.

During the last days of Jewish Palestine, Golda tried to persuade the Jewish terrorist gangs to stop blowing up British properties, and especially to stop terrorizing the Jews themselves in order to acquire money. The gangs retaliated by declaring Golda Meyerson a traitor. She gained the respect of most Jews for not going into hiding.

Still determined to bring as many Jews into Palestine as possible, Golda made a trip to Cyprus. There, in the refugee camps where the

British were detaining concentration camp survivors, she persuaded many people to give their precious places in the immigration line to children so that at least the young ones could be taken to Palestine.

THE VOTE

Day by day, radio broadcast by radio broadcast, the Jews—and indeed the world—followed the ups and downs of the UN's arguments about partition of Palestine. The UN was meeting in the small town of Lake Success, New York, where the Sperry Gyroscope Company had donated space to be used while a permanent UN headquarters was planned.

On November 29, 1947, the fifty-seven member nations of the UN General Assembly voted to end the twenty-seven-year-old British Mandate and to recommend that Palestine be divided into a Jewish state and an Arab state. Thirty-three member nations voted in favor; thirteen (mostly Arab) nations voted against; and ten nations, including Britain, abstained. The partition was to take effect on August 1, 1948.

As the news was reported on the radio, the Jews and even some British soldiers began to celebrate. Golda spoke from the balcony of her Histadrut office, primarily to angry Arabs who swirled through the crowd. She said she knew that the plan was a compromise, but perhaps the long-time enemies could now live in friendship and peace.

But Golda knew that while there would soon be a nation of Israel, there would also be a war, perhaps to the death.

CHAPTER SEVEN

Working for Her New Country

G olda's eyes filled with tears when David Ben-Gurion spoke the words "the State of Israel" during the independence ceremony on May 14, 1948, or, according to the Jewish calendar, fifth of Lyar, 5708.

> ## We had done it . . . .We had brought the Jewish state into existence—and I, Golda Mabovitch Meyerson, had lived to see the day. Whatever . . . price any of us would have to pay for it, we had re-created the Jewish national home. The long exile was over.

Only two women signed the Proclamation of Independence. One was Rachel Kagan, a 1919 immigrant who founded the Women's International Zionist Organization and an avid speaker in support of women's suffrage. The other was Golda Meyerson. Golda was also the only leader of Israel to have come from the United States. U.S. president Harry Truman immediately granted tiny Israel the formal recognition of the United States, probably for two reasons. As a believer in the Bible, he felt that

Golda Meyerson, who would soon take the Hebrew name Meir, is shown shaking hands with David Ben-Gurion when it seemed that Israel would become a nation.

the Jews deserved their own state, and he wanted the support of Jewish voters in the upcoming 1948 presidential elections.

THE WAR OF INDEPENDENCE

As in the history of the United States, just declaring independence did not enact it. The old British Mandate would end at midnight on May 14, and there would no longer be British soldiers in Israel. It was up to the new nation to defend itself.

Virtually within hours after midnight, Egyptian fighter planes were seen in the sky, and troops from Egypt, Syria, Jordan, Iraq, and Lebanon were swarming over the borders. Both sides were determined to gain the ancient city of Jerusalem. For Jews, reclaiming that city would bring fruition to the prayer "next year in Jerusalem," which Jews had spoken at their Seder dinners on Passover every year for hundreds of years.

The war for Jerusalem actually had started some months before, when the UN had passed the resolution to partition Palestine. Jerusalem was under siege; the Arabs attacked any convoys carrying goods into the city by the main road. Buildings in Jerusalem were blown up. None of these attacks were bad enough to spur the British troops to help the Jews. When Arabs took the Old City, they destroyed the Jewish Quarter. The siege was broken when Jewish laborers managed to build a rough road to Tel Aviv along a different route. Convoys could once again carry supplies to the city.

The Jews knew that these attacks were just the prelude to a genuine, full-fledged war. They needed a huge amount of money to buy weapons. In the past, they had stolen all their weapons or built them in Haganah factories. But those weapons were not enough to fight a full-out modern war against the Arabs. Once again, the only source of the money they needed was the Jews of America.

The executive council knew that David Ben-Gurion, the public symbol of their forthcoming nation, must not leave Israel just as it had come into existence. They sent Golda Meyerson instead.

American Jews did not welcome Golda with open arms. Most of them were not Zionists; they did not believe that it was necessary for Jews to have a homeland. She told her audiences,

There is no Jew in Palestine who does not believe that finally we will be victorious. That is the spirit of the country. . . . Rifles and machine guns without spirit are not worth very much, but spirit without arms can, in time, be broken together with the body.

Golda spoke everywhere that Jews would listen. One speech, made in Chicago on January 2, 1948, brought in so much money that it has been called "the speech that made possible a Jewish state." That one stop in Golda's six weeks of travels brought in a phenomenal $75 million. Upon Golda's return, Ben-Gurion said,

Someday when history will be written, it will be said that there was a Jewish woman who got the money which made the state possible.

AMBASSADOR MEYERSON

While in the United States, Golda learned that she had been made Israel's ambassador to the Soviet Union. She had no desire to move there. After all, she now lived in a new nation and wasn't ready to leave it, certainly not for Russia, which only represented horrible childhood memories. As usual, however, she was prepared to do what her people asked. Before she left New York, however, she broke her leg in a taxicab accident and was hospitalized for several weeks. She returned to Israel before she should have, and then she went on to Moscow.

Ambassador Meyerson spent only seven months in Moscow, but those months changed the lives of Jews in Russia. Many Jews enthusiastically demonstrated upon her arrival, but that caused the anti-religious communist government to crack down on all public exhibitions of Jewish culture. Soviet leaders did not want to know that there were still Jews—especially young ones—with a yearning for Zion. Ironically, the wife of the Soviet foreign minister, Vyacheslav Molotov, was Jewish. At a reception, she startled Golda by speaking to her in Yiddish. Later she was arrested and imprisoned until the death of dictator Joseph Stalin four years later.

MINISTER OF LABOR

Israel held its first parliamentary elections while Golda was in Moscow. Golda's party, Mapai, won most of the seats in the Knesset, Israeli's legislative body (the *K* is pronounced: kuh-ness-it). The Knesset's 120 members, called *haverim*, are elected. The government is a parliamentary system, meaning that the voters choose their haverim, and then their haverim select the prime minister.

Ambassador Golda Meir and her daughter, Sarah, departing for Russia

Israel's first president (an honorary position) was Chaim Weiz-mann. The Knesset chose David Ben-Gurion as the first prime minis-ter, and Ben-Gurion asked Golda to return to Israel to take the position of minister of labor. The religious faction in the government opposed the idea of a woman cabinet minister, but they finally accepted the argument that since there had been a female judge named Deborah in ancient Israel, it would be all right to choose Golda. From then on, Gol-da served as an ally of Ben-Gurion in every Israeli cabinet until 1965.

When the UN announced its plan for partitioning Palestine and forming a Jewish nation, Jews from such countries as China, Algeria, and Poland began to move into Palestine. Unlike the Jews of earlier years, most of them were destitute, and it was up to the Histadrut to find them homes and jobs and to make sure they learned Hebrew.

Immigrants continued to arrive regardless of the fact that the War of Independence continued month after month. Israel lost about 6,300 people, about one-third of whom were soldiers—more than one percent of the population.

Israel and the neighboring Arab countries made separate armistice agreements in 1949. These nearby nations included Egypt, Lebanon, Jordan, and Syria. The agreements established new borders but left Egypt occupying Gaza, a narrow strip of land bordering the Mediterranean Sea at Egypt's Sinai Peninsula. The war also left Jordan occupying the West Bank. The West Bank, which the Israelis call Judea and Samaria, is the land west of the Jordan River that Jordan had captured and continued to control for forty years. These agreements were not peace treaties; they just settled the short War of Independence. They certainly did not stop the Arab-Israeli wars, which continue to this day.

THE NEW IMMIGRANTS

Golda held the position of labor minister for seven years. It was her responsibility to find useful work for the hundreds of thousands of Jews pouring into the new Jewish state every year. She also had to find permanent homes for them.

In July 1950 the Knesset passed the Law of Return. It gave all Jews anywhere the right to immigrate to Israel and gave them automatic Israeli citizenship.

Muslims throughout the Middle East had protested the partition plan. The biggest riot occurred in Aden, the capital of Yemen. The Jews of Yemen soon found themselves unable to keep their poverty-stricken society going. Many of them set out to walk to Israel. The Israelis, helped by Americans, secretly collected and flew almost

50,000 Yemenite Jews into the new nation in 1950. The event was officially called Operation Wings of Eagles, but people have since called it Operation Magic Carpet.

The Yemenite rescue was just the first of many similar operations. Another was Operation Ali Baba, in which 113,000 Jews were airlifted to Israel from Iraq. Soon there were tent cities holding hundreds of thousands of new immigrants from at least seventy countries. The tiny nation's population doubled in less than two years.

These immigrants were not robust men and women prepared to work hard. They were extremely poor, usually uneducated and untrained, and often diseased. They spoke many different languages. Golda was responsible for turning them into Israelis. In order for the tiny country to handle all these people, all Israelis had to ration food and clothing. They could not have all they wanted—only what was available to be shared. This period of austerity lasted more than ten years.

Again Golda went to the United States to raise funds to help Israel survive. And again, the Jews in the United States were generous. With the money, Golda organized the immigrants to help build thousands of simple homes in villages all over Israel. She also organized the building of roads between the villages; this put many thousands more immigrants to work.

Golda became adept at using whatever funds were available to educate and to train thousands of people. Some immigrants never overcame their limitations, but many others learned new skills at the vocational training centers Golda established.

In the midst of all her labor, Golda received word that her husband, Morris Meyerson, had died—ironically, in Golda's own home. She hurried home and attended his funeral. She felt sorrowful that they had had such a self-destructive life both together and apart.

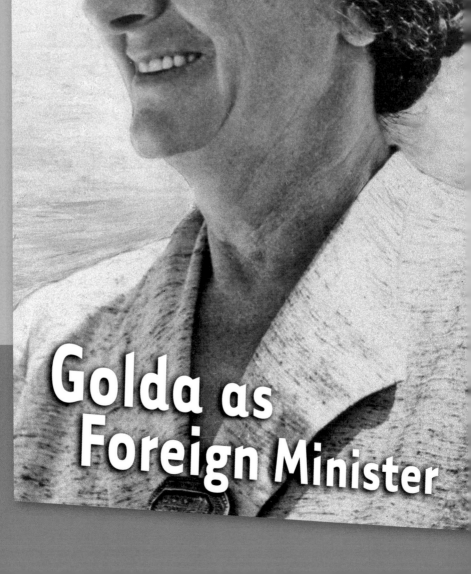

CHAPTER EIGHT

Golda as
Foreign Minister

B Y 1956, PRIME MINISTER BEN-GURION and his foreign minister, Moshe Sharett, had increasingly different views on how Israel should be run. Ben-Gurion felt that the Israeli government needed to consider only what would be good for Israel. Sharett, on the other hand, thought it was equally important to consider how the rest of the world would view any actions they took. Ultimately, Ben-Gurion dismissed Sharett and gave him the post of secretary-general of the Mapai party. He asked Golda Meyerson to take the job of foreign minister.

Although some of the people who signed the Proclamation of Independence had used Hebrew versions of their names, Golda Meyerson had not. But Ben-Gurion wanted her to change her name to something Hebrew so that she could better represent Israel abroad. Golda chose Meir, which means "illuminate," because it was fairly close to Meyerson. Ever after, she was known as Golda Meir, though it took her a while to get used to her new name.

People who were involved in international affairs all over the world came to trust Foreign Minister Golda Meir and to accept both her tears and her sternness as part of her character. Everything she did in her ten years as foreign minister hinged on whether a certain action or decision would be good or bad for Israel. Much of what Israel became in those years was a result

Golda Meir, Israeli Minister of Foreign Affairs

of this criterion. In his book *Golda Meir: Portrait of a Prime Minister*, Israeli author Eliyahu Agress writes,

Her appearance on the international stage gave the impression—as it still does—that this woman bore on her shoulders the two thousand years of Jewish dispersion and was suffused with the burning faith in the justice of her cause.

SUEZ AND SINAI

As the years passed, Golda's country was regularly invaded by fedayeen, the Arab fighters financed by Egypt's leader, Gamal Abdel Nasser, to murder, to rob, and generally to bring down Israel. The fedayeen operated primarily from the Gaza Strip. According to the UN's 1947 partition plan, the Gaza Strip was to be part of an eventual Arab state. After the War of Independence, Egypt controlled the area. The Egyptian government's policy was to keep the Arab refugees living in Gaza destitute so that they could blame their inhuman situation on Israel.

In July 1956 Egypt abruptly took over the Suez Canal, which had been built by the French in 1869 but run by the British. The British, French, and Israelis planned what came to be called the Sinai Campaign to regain control of the canal. Golda secretly flew to France to help organize the campaign. Until the date of the planned attack, she was unable to tell anyone—even her immediate family—about the plan. She found it difficult to play with her grandchildren as if nothing momentous was about to happen.

The French were allies of the Israelis, and Golda worked with them on the development of nuclear power and nuclear weaponry. What started out as a power plant in the Israeli desert probably turned into nuclear weapons ready for use, though they have never been used and their existence has never been confirmed.

On October 29, 1956, Israeli troops invaded the Sinai and overran Gaza with the help of the British and French. Concerned that the Soviet Union would become involved, U.S. leaders forced a quick cease-fire by threatening to withhold oil supplies, which the United States controlled at that time.

AIMING FOR PEACE

On March 1, 1957, Golda Meir, as Israeli foreign minister, spoke before the General Assembly of the United Nations. She was speaking directly to the representatives of the Arab nations when she said,

> Can we, from now on—all of us—turn a new leaf and, instead of fighting with each other, can we all, united, fight poverty and disease and illiteracy? Is it possible for us to put all our efforts and all our energy into one single purpose, the betterment and progress and development of all our lands and all our peoples?

But no one in the great hall was willing to help Israel. The tiny young nation was forced to withdraw from the territories that might have given them a buffer. Egyptian troops returned to Gaza and kept the area quiet until 2000. UN peacekeeping forces occupied the Sinai for the coming years.

On each of Golda's visits to the UN, she tried to make a breakthrough with the Arabs, but nothing ever came of her efforts. Even leaders of other countries, when they held receptions in New York City, could not invite representatives from both Israel and Arab countries to the same functions.

If she couldn't communicate with Arabs in Israel's neighborhood, Golda decided, she would find Muslims elsewhere and befriend them. She made her first trip to Africa in early 1958 and visited a number of newly independent countries that were just learning to run themselves. Some of them were primarily Muslim, and she introduced Israel as friend rather than as enemy. In Liberia, the Gola tribe crowned Golda their queen, or, more officially, their paramount chief. During one ceremony, Golda, wearing formal robes, was presented with a live chicken. Each year she traveled thousands of miles through Africa. She helped the former colonies in every way she and her Israeli agricultural specialists could. In turn, many African leaders visited Israel.

When colleagues challenged her about why Israelis should pay so much attention to Africa, Golda replied, referring to the president of Egypt,

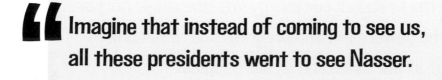 Imagine that instead of coming to see us, all these presidents went to see Nasser.

Adolf Eichmann, Nazi war criminal, behind a protective glass shield during his 1961 trial in Jerusalem

GOLDA AND EICHMANN

Adolf Eichmann was a German Nazi officer who had been responsible for moving Jews from all over Europe to extermination camps. As the war ended, American troops captured Eichmann, but they didn't realize how important he was. He managed to escape and eventually reached Argentina. After the war, many Jews dedicated themselves to finding and exposing Nazis. Mossad, the Israeli intelligence agency, located Eichmann in 1960 and captured him. Golda handled the negotiations with Argentina to transfer him to Israel for trial.

When Argentina condemned Israel for kidnapping an Argentinean resident, Golda had to speak before the UN Security Council to explain what the trial meant to Jews. She also had to guarantee that the kidnapping of Eichmann was an isolated incident, and Israel would not make a habit of it.

The Israelis didn't want just to execute Eichmann for his crimes against the Jews. They wanted the world to hear what he had done. In 1961, with the world watching on television, Eichmann was tried in a public court. Throughout the long trial he sat inside a booth made of bulletproof glass. After fourteen weeks of testimony, the former Nazi was found guilty. He was executed on May 31, 1962, in the only death penalty ever carried out in Israel.

GOLDA AND THE ARABS

Golda knew that Israel would never be able to live in peace if its Arab neighbors continued to deny its right to exist. In late 1960, in a speech to the UN General Assembly, she challenged Arab countries to send leaders to meet with Prime Minister Ben-Gurion. They would seek a peace settlement and negotiate a way to handle the Arab refugees. Nasser replied, "Never!" He also said that there would never be a solution to the Arab refugee problem as long as Israel existed.

In 1963, the League of Arab States (the Arab League) formed the Palestine Liberation Organization (PLO). In later years, Yasser Arafat, founder of the Fatah political party, became the leader of the PLO and the most recognizable Arab face in the Middle East. PLO guerrillas infiltrated Israel from surrounding lands to make frequent terrorist

The Golan Heights is a strategically important plateau that lies within or straddles the borders of Syria, Israel, Lebanon, and Jordan. Israel currently controls the region.

attacks against civilians. In addition, the Syrian army often launched artillery from the Golan Heights toward nearby kibbutzim. The Soviet Union supported all of these efforts.

That same year, Golda met with U. S. president John F. Kennedy. She explained to him how important it was to the world's Jews to keep Israel alive. He listened intently and then said,

**" I understand, Mrs. Meir. Don't worry.
Nothing will happen to Israel. "**

Of course, Kennedy was unable to keep his promise, because he himself was assassinated soon afterward. And Mrs. Meir herself retired from her position as foreign minister.

CHAPTER NINE

A New Life

B Y 1965, GOLDA WAS EXPERIENCING FREQUENT migraine headaches and was exhausted from all her travels. She was sixty-seven years old and had worked continuously, often for twenty-hour days, for most of her life. Levi Eshkol, the prime minister, tried to keep her in his cabinet as deputy prime minister, but she turned down the position. She was looking forward to relaxing with her sister, Sheyna, and getting to know her grandchildren better.

Golda designed a duplex in a suburb of Tel Aviv and shared it with her son, Menachem, and his family. She even enjoyed doing her own shopping and taking public transportation instead of being driven everywhere.

But this peaceful life wouldn't last. Mapai was in trouble. Split into several factions, the party could neither function nor win elections. Mapai leaders asked Golda to come back to work as the party's secretary-general and to build bridges among the factions. She had worked her entire life for the party that emphasized the importance of labor. She could not see the party fail now. She returned to work.

Many members of the Knesset did not trust Levi Eshkol, the Mapai prime minister, who was also the defense minister in 1967. The major leaders of all the political parties gathered in a coalition government that would take over. They asked David Ben-Gurion, who had retired, if he would come back and head the government. Reluctantly, he agreed. Some of the party leaders wanted Moshe Dayan, a famous soldier, to become defense

Golda Meir took great pride in casting her vote in the elections of her new Jewish nation.

minister, but Golda, among others, objected. She was outnumbered, and Dayan became defense minister under a unity government that joined the major parties to face the national emergency of war. The cabinet members hoped that the public would be encouraged by Dayan's appointment as defense minister because, once again, Arab troops were gathering on Israel's borders and war seemed inevitable.

THE SIX-DAY WAR

On May 18, 1967, Egypt expelled UN troops who had been in the Sinai Peninsula since 1957. When the UN did not complain about the act, Egypt felt free to make other moves. Egyptian tanks moved to the Israeli border and cut off Israel's access to the Strait of Tiran, which is the only way for Israelis to reach the Red Sea. By international law, this was an act of war.

Golda, no longer a member of the cabinet, could only watch, wait, and prepare for the assault. This time, Israelis did everything possible to prepare as tension mounted, day by day. The surrounding Arab countries held massive demonstrations calling for the end of the Jews and Israel. Israel responded by consecrating the land in public parks in case it would be needed for mass cemeteries.

Finally, on June 5, Israel, under Defense Minister Moshe Dayan, struck first by destroying most of Egypt's airforce. Arab troops moved into Israel from all directions.

The war did indeed last six days. Once again, it was primarily Egypt, Syria, and Jordan against Israel. The Soviet Union backed the Arab nations, and the United States remained officially neutral. On the third day, the Israelis captured the whole of Jerusalem. They found that, during the years of Arab control of the Old City, syna-

GOLDA AT THE WALL

The Western Wall in Jerusalem is the only part of Solomon's two-thousand-year-old temple still visible in Jerusalem. It is sometimes called the Wailing Wall because by tradition Jews go to it and weep for the destruction of the temple. A section less than 200 feet [61 meters] long is exposed on Temple Mount. More of the wall still exists, but houses block access to it.

On the third day of the Six-Day War, Jewish soldiers freed the Old City of Jerusalem, and for the first time in nineteen years, Jews were able to go to the Western Wall. Ordinary citizens were not yet free to visit it because fighting was still going on in the city, but Golda was allowed in. She saw the soldiers who had liberated the ancient city crying at the wall and inserting *kuitlech*, or notes of prayer, into the cracks. This woman, who was not raised as a pious Jew, later said of that day that she finally understood the importance of the ancient wall to Jews: "I saw a nation's refusal to accept that only these stones were left to it and an expression of confidence in what was to come in the future."

gogues had been destroyed and Jewish tombstones had been used to pave the floors of latrines.

On the next day, the Israelis captured the West Bank, which had been in Jordan's hands. On the sixth day, Israel captured the Golan Heights from Syria. The Arab armies were defeated. The war was over.

The war left Israel four times larger than it had been. Israel took control of the Sinai Peninsula, the Gaza Strip, the West Bank, the

Golan Heights, and East Jerusalem. The UN Security Council passed Resolution 242. Although people have debated the document's exact interpretation, most of the international politicians involved felt that it did not require Israel to give up the lands it had captured. However, gradually, over the intervening years, Israel has given up most of the captured territory.

Golda Meir was seventy years old and in poor health. She continued to travel as much as she could during the following years. When she spoke in public she had an uncanny ability to perceive which aspects of her own story a particular audience would find most enticing. With one audience she would emphasize her Russian background; with another she would highlight her experience as an immigrant in Milwaukee. Another group might find her early years in Palestine fascinating. She managed to make each audience feel as if she was telling her story just to them.

Golda was at home in her Tel Aviv suburb on February 26, 1969, when Prime Minister Levi Eshkol died suddenly of a heart attack.

The cabinet held an emergency meeting to choose a new prime minister. Golda Meir's name was the only one that did not bring up huge objections. One man speaking in favor of her nomination said, "I feel that Golda is hewn from the rock that this mission demands. She is endowed with the traits that this post demands. Her personality carries the required authority; her political experience is unusually rich; her standing among Jews of the world is incomparable . . . and she has it in her to engender the spirit of genuine coalition."

Golda was dismayed at the very idea. After all, she was retired and had no desire to go back to work. Also, she knew that she wasn't very popular with the general public, certainly not as popular as Defense Minister Moshe Dayan. However, she soon began to accept that she could at least serve as interim prime minister until elections could

THE IRON GRANDMOTHER

In 2008, Julia Baird of *Newsweek* looked back at the early female leaders. "The pursuit of power is rarely pretty. The first few female leaders were considered so unusual, they were cast as male, or metal. In the 1960s and '70s, Iron Ladies sprang up around the globe, breathing fire—Indira Gandhi in 1966, Golda Meir in 1969, Thatcher in 1979—women who did not shy from war and quashed any notion that women were the gentler sex. Their success created one of the most repetitive clichés for women in politics—iron maidens, iron butterflies, even steel magnolias—as journalists cooed over the fact that a woman could be (gasp!) decisive and authoritative, a marvelous combination of flesh and steel."

be held the following October. She later recalled, "I was dazed. I had never planned to be prime minister; I had never planned any position, in fact. I had planned to come to Palestine, to go to Merhavia, to be active in the labor movement. But the position I would occupy? That never."

On March 17, 1969, Golda Meir stepped out of the main body of the Knesset and was sworn in as prime minister. Apparently everyone in the parliament wanted to be heard on that day. The speeches given in honor of their new leader lasted five hours.

CHAPTER TEN

The Prime Minister

THE WORLD NEWS MEDIA DESCRIBED ISRAEL'S new prime minister as grandmotherly. Gray-haired, seventy-two-year-old Golda Meir was indeed a grandmother. However, grandmothers, often thought of as warm and cozy, can be manipulative. They can work subtly to get a person to do what they want. And that's what "the sassy nicotine-stained grandmother who wore baggy suits and orthopedic shoes" was good at.

Other women had preceded Golda as prime ministers of their countries. However, each had reached the position through family connections—Sirimavo Bandaranaike of Sri Lanka followed her husband in 1960, and Indira Gandhi followed her father, Prime Minister Jawaharlal Nehru, in 1966. Golda Meir was elected on her own, with no family member paving the way.

When Prime Minister Golda Meir visited the United States soon after she was sworn in, everyone who thought they had a reason to be in her presence was excited. Dinners and parties were given for her everywhere. The *New York Times* accused New York City mayor John Lindsay of throwing the most lavish party ever held by the city for a public figure. Another dinner in New York included almost three thousand Jewish leaders from throughout the United States.

In Washington, D.C., Prime Minister Meir hoped to negotiate major weapons from the United States. At the same time, William Rogers, who was President Nixon's secretary of state, was trying to get Israel to withdraw from the land it had occupied

Prime Minister Golda Meir, who learned to give speeches in the streets of Milwaukee, never held back her opinions.

since 1967. Golda refused even to consider that. Nixon himself found Golda charming, and he called her a strong, intelligent leader. He agreed with Ben-Gurion's assessment—that Golda was the "best man" in his cabinet—a phrase that Golda hated.

When an American newspaper reporter asked Golda if being a woman was ever a handicap to her, she replied that she didn't know since she had never tried being a man.

THE WAR LEADER

Golda left her friendly suburban home and moved into the prime minister's official residence in Jerusalem. The first official order she gave might be called grandmotherly—she was to be notified, day or night, whenever there were casualties among Israel's soldiers. She also immediately notified the leaders of neighboring Arab countries that she was willing to discuss peace. A Jordanian newspaper reported,

 Golda Meir is behaving like a grandmother telling bedtime stories to her grandchildren.

As prime minister, Golda generally spent the first part of the workweek in Jerusalem, the latter part in Tel Aviv, and the weekend at her home in Ramat Aviv. Everyone had a chance to meet with her, and she kept tabs on everything that was happening in her country.

Even though the Six-Day War was over, the fighting had not stopped. The Soviet Union had rebuilt the equipment and supplies of

Egypt, so that the Egyptians could attack Israel continuously. The perpetual attacks were never enough to constitute a full-scale war, but they were definitely enough for the Arabs to hope that Israel would rethink keeping control of the Sinai Peninsula from the Israeli border to the Suez Canal.

Egypt could afford to lose many men. The much smaller nation of Israel could not. The new prime minister decided that it was time to put a stop to Egypt's war of attrition, which it carried out in little attacks here and there. She called her new policy asymmetrical response. Whenever Egypt struck at Israel, she struck back in a much larger, more devastating way.

It worked. After Nasser's death in 1970, the new Egyptian president, Anwar Sadat, ceased the overt pinprick attacks on Israel. Instead, he began to rebuild his army behind the scenes and to plan for a bigger war.

Because they had won the War of Independence and the Six-Day War, Golda and those around her were certain, at least subconsciously, that little Israel would always be able to best its larger neighbors in war. After all, they were fighting for survival, while their enemies were not.

Golda's cabinet was often called the Kitchen Cabinet, because she often met with her closest advisers in her kitchen. She ran her cabinet very tightly, with an "iron fist." Her cabinet members never outvoted her. People often criticized Golda for so tightly controlling her cabinet, as they felt she should surround herself with diverse opinions.

In 1970 the UN Security Council proposed a peace plan that would prevent Israel from negotiating directly with Egypt. Golda, as well as others in the Knesset, rejected the plan.

And apparently nothing would stop the neighboring Arabs.

THE YOM KIPPUR WAR

It was October 1973. Arab troops had been gathering on Israeli borders for some months, particularly the Syrians on the Golan Heights on the border north of the Sea of Galilee (also called Lake Tiberias). But Golda's Kitchen Cabinet did not think that another war was about to start. Israeli intelligence personnel were certain that the whole buildup was designed strictly to make the Israelis *think* there was about to be a war, not that there was actually going to be one.

On Friday evening, October 5, the most sacred of Jewish holidays—Yom Kippur, the Day of Atonement—began at dusk. For the following twenty-five hours, Israel would virtually shut down for fasting and prayer. Even for nonreligious Jews, nothing would function in the ordinary way.

Just hours before the start of Yom Kippur, Golda received news that the Russian advisors to the Syrian troops were hurriedly leaving the Golan Heights. She feared that something was about to happen. The military officials around her did not think the news meant anything, but she called all cabinet ministers who were in Tel Aviv to a Friday meeting. The ministers, too, thought nothing was about to happen, but they agreed to support her if she suddenly had to call up the troops during the holiday.

Golda remembered the previous May when the troops had been called up, and nothing had happened. It had been a great expense and alarm for nothing. So she continued to hesitate, counting on sufficient advance warning if an attack really were to happen.

Then they did get a warning, but they had only hours to call up the reserve forces before the Egyptians and Syrians, along with some troops from Jordan and Iraq, attacked the next day along two fronts. Golda turned down the suggestion that the air force strike first, as it had when the Six-Day War started. Because it was Yom Kippur, many of the troops could not be reached, and only a partial army was in place to react when the war started at noon.

> **For me, that fact cannot and never will be erased, and there can be no consolation in anything that anyone else has to say or in all of the commonsense rationalizations with which my colleagues have tried to comfort me. . . . I will never again be the person I was before the Yom Kippur War.**

Enemy forces attacked from the south, from the Suez Canal area in Egypt, and from the north in the Golan Heights. Israeli solders were dying by the hundreds as the days went on, but the prime minister had to go on radio and television to tell her people that the government had done their "best to prevent the outbreak."

Golda asked the Americans for help. President Nixon had promised her assistance, but he was in the midst of the Watergate scandal, which would result in his resigning the presidency. And now the U.S. Department of Defense was hesitating, even though they saw that the Soviet Union was helping the Syrians and the Egyptians. Finally, on October 14, military supplies such as tanks, ammunition, and rockets began to arrive by massive airlift from the United States. This airlift, called Operation Nickel Grass, has been heralded as saving Israel.

CEASE-FIRE

When she spoke before the Knesset on October 16, Prime Minister Meir was speaking to the world. People had always criticized Israel for not withdrawing to the lines that existed before the Six-Day War. She was able to point out that, if the Israelis had withdrawn, this new war might have been their final, losing war. Israel, the Jewish homeland, would exist no more.

By October 19 it was clear that Syria and the Egyptians were losing. Once again little Israel was beating the larger nations around it. The Soviet Union rushed its diplomats in to encourage a cease-fire. In the end, Henry Kissinger of the United States and Leonid Brezhnev of the Soviet Union arranged it. Golda wrote, "In the final analysis, to put it bluntly, the fate of small countries always rests with the superpowers, and they always have their own interests to guard."

The UN Security Council hurriedly passed a cease-fire that prevented the Syrian and Egyptian armies from being completely destroyed. The resolution called for establishing a "just and durable peace in the Middle East." But Golda had no feeling that such a peace could happen. Then the Syrians rejected the cease-fire. The fighting went on.

A new cease-fire was planned. Golda held out so she could negotiate keeping the land Israel had entered in Syria to put a safety buffer around the settlements near the border. And still the talks went on for long, harrowing days until, on November 11, 1973, the new cease-fire went into effect. Golda knew that the final agreement reflected the powerful nations' desires, especially the U.S. leaders' desire to not jeopardize oil resources. But Golda was glad when Israeli soldiers sat down with Egyptian soldiers for the first time in twenty-five years, and prisoners were exchanged.

Only a few weeks later, on December 1, David Ben-Gurion died in Tel Aviv. The body of the Founding Father of Israel lay in state for millions of mourners to pass by. U.S. president Richard Nixon said, "With courage, love, and determination, David Ben-Gurion worked to establish the modern State of Israel. As we move forward in the struggle for justice and peace, we take from the example of his life increased conviction that cause will triumph."

BLAMING GOLDA

Immediately, Israelis started complaining about the Meir government. They *should* have expected an attack, they *should* have been prepared. The deaths of 2,500 young men and women lay at her feet, the fault of her lack of preparedness. The Israeli Supreme Court president was asked to lead an investigation. His report found several intelligence officers responsible. Golda Meir and Defense Minister Moshe Dayan were cleared, but the public was not willing to accept that decision.

Even in the midst of the criticism, Israel held an election, and the coalition of party factions that had chosen Golda Meir as prime minister was kept in power. However, Golda had great difficulty putting a government together. There were too many factions, even in her own party, that insisted on being represented.

On April 11, 1974, Golda reached her own limit, physically, emotionally, and mentally. She formally resigned as prime minister. But even then she wasn't through—she had to stay in office, as caretaker, until a new government could be formed under Yitzhak Rabin. He was the first Israeli prime minister to be a Sabra—someone born in Israel.

Golda Meir left office on June 4, knowing that finally an agreement had been reached with Syria and that Israeli prisoners of war would be coming home.

The prisoners were coming home to a land that had grown in Golda's lifetime from a mere 80,000 Jews in Palestine in the 1920s to 3 million residents of a new nation, Israel. More than one-third of Israel's citizens had come to the Jewish homeland from locations all over the earth.

CHAPTER ELEVEN

The Last Days

A fter she relinquished the reins of power, there were two views of Golda Meir. The American view was that she was an idealist who had held together a new nation. The Israeli view, after the Yom Kippur War, was that she had failed her people in their time of need.

Returning to her own home, the ailing Golda worked on her autobiography. *My Life* was published in 1975. It became an immediate best seller in countries all over the world because everyone wanted to know what Golda thought of herself. The book revealed how torn she always was between her public persona, which she saw as successful, and her private life, which she viewed as very unsuccessful because of her failed marriage and the emotional distance between her and her children.

Amos Elon, writing in the *New York Times* review of Golda's autobiography, described her as

the very personification of the Jews' will to survive as a people in the aftermath of the Nazi holocaust and in the face of repeated Arab attacks.

The interest aroused by Golda's autobiography prompted playwright William Gibson to write *Golda*, a two-act play that starred actress Anne Bancroft on Broadway. Theatrical

Her life dedicated to the Jewish homeland,
Golda Meir died there in 1978.

reviewer Margaret Croyden went to Israel with Anne Bancroft to meet Golda. She found the prime minister "a tough-minded, commanding presence who admirably represented the pioneer spirit of the Zionists in the early days of Israel's independence. True to her beliefs, she lived a pioneer's life without any trimmings. The Israeli Prime Minister's quarters was a three-room, little house with a garden in the backyard. . . . Golda did not surround herself with glamour or convenience; she wore no makeup, dressed like an ordinary housewife about to go shopping at the local grocery store, and reminded me (sometimes) of all the Jewish women in my family."

The play opened on November 14 with the real Golda in the audience, but she hurried home at the end. Anwar Sadat, the president of Egypt, had startled the world when he suddenly decided to go to Jerusalem in November 1977 in the hopes of pushing the peace process forward. The first person Sadat met was Golda Meir. Speaking before the Israeli Knesset, he urged Jews, as well as Arabs, to break through their determination never to give up anything. Sadat was hopeful, but Israeli prime minister Menachem Begin refused to yield on the issue of giving up the West Bank. He was willing to grant self-rule to the Arabs who lived there, but Israel would retain control of both land and water.

A weak but still determined eighty-year-old Golda also spoke to the Knesset. She said directly to Sadat, "Mr. President, we have a saying in Hebrew: 'zchut rishonim.' In English, this means 'the privilege of being the first.' I congratulate you, Mr. President, that you are privileged to be the first great Arab leader of the greatest country among our neighbors to come to us, with courage and determination, despite so many difficulties, for the sake of your sons, as well as for the sake of ours; for the sake of all mothers who mourn sons that fell in battle."

A few months later, the two sides went to Camp David, Maryland, the U.S. presidential retreat, and worked out an agreement, overseen by President Jimmy Carter. For that effort, called the Camp David Accords, Menachem Begin and Anwar Sadat received the Nobel Peace Prize of 1978.

REMEMBERING

On December 8, 1978, as Begin and Sadat were celebrating their Nobel Peace Prize in Oslo, Norway, Golda Meir died. She had been in and out of the hospital for weeks. She was buried on Mount Herzl in Jerusalem.

The following year, Egypt and Israel signed an actual peace treaty. It was the first time that an Arab country had acknowledged the existence of Israel. Sadat gradually lost most of his support in Egypt, and in 1981, Islamic radicals assassinated him during a celebration of Egypt's "successes" in the Yom Kippur War.

Golda always remained Golda, and even today, if the name Golda is said, people in many Jewish communities know who is meant. People around the world remained interested in her. Elinor Burkett, a university history professor and journalist, published a new biography and study of Golda in 2008. In the United States, the book was called simply *Golda*, But in Great Britain it was called *Golda: The Iron Lady of the Middle East*. In the book's conclusion, Burkett describes Golda not so much as an iron lady as a tragic figure. Israelis turned on her after all she had done for the Jewish nation. A lonely woman, she had been so busy working that she never cultivated friendships. All her efforts, her entire life, were directed toward the Jewish homeland to which she first moved as a young woman. And in those efforts, Golda never wavered.

TIMELINE

1898 — Born in Kiev, Russia (now Ukraine)

1906 — Family moves to the United States, settling in Milwaukee

1914 — Runs away to sister in Denver, Colorado

1916 — Graduates from North Division High School in Milwaukee

1917 — Marries Morris Meyerson

1921 — Meyerson family arrives in Palestine

1926 — Begins to work for the Histadrut

1934 — Joins the Yishuv Executive Council

1946 — Becomes acting head of the political department of the government

1948 — Appointed Israel's first ambassador to the Soviet Union

1949	Elected to the Knesset, the parliament
1949–1956	Serves as minister of labor and national insurance
1956–1966	Serves as minister of foreign affairs
1966–1968	Chosen to lead the major political party, Mapai
1969	Chosen to succeed Levi Eshkol as prime minister
1973	Yom Kippur War
1974	Resigns her position as prime minister
1975	Awarded Israel Prize
1975	Autobiography, *My Life*, published
1978	Dies in Jerusalem

SOURCE NOTES

Boxed quotes unless otherwise noted

CHAPTER 1

p. 5, Golda Meir, *My Life* (New York: Putnam, 1975), pp. 13–14.

CHAPTER 2

p. 18, Ralph G. Martin, *Golda: The Romantic Years* (New York: Scribner, 1988), p. 66.

p. 19, par. 3, Elinor Burkett, *Golda* (New York: HarperCollins, 2008), quoted on page 37, apparently from Israel State Archives.

CHAPTER 3

p. 33, par. 1, David Ben-Gurion, *Days of David Ben-Gurion* (New York: Grossman Publishers, 1967), p. 13.

p. 33, par. 4, *My Life*, p. 119.

CHAPTER 4

p. 42, *My Life*, p. 113.

p. 47, Shulamit Reinharz and Mark A. Raider, *American Jewish Women and the Zionist Enterprise* (Hanover, NH: UPNE, 2005), p. 115.

p. 49, Martin, p. x

CHAPTER 5

p. 51, par. 3, *My Life*, pp. 142–43.

p. 55, par. 2, *My Life*, p. 157.

p. 55-56, par. 4-par. 1, *My Life*, p. 158.

p. 57, par. 3, Online Christian Action for Israel article on the Evian Conference, quoting the *Manchester Guardian*. www.christianactionforisrael.org

CHAPTER 6

p. 60, Online Israel Ministry of Foreign Affairs biography of Ben-Gurion. www.mfa.gov.il/MFA

p. 65, *My Life*, p. 199.

p. 66, par. 3, Novelist Leon Uris tells the story of the *Exodus* in a 1958 novel. It was made into a very popular film, *Exodus*, by Otto Preminger in 1960.

p. 66, *My Life*, p. 207.

CHAPTER 7

p. 71, *My Life*, p. 226.

p. 73, *My Life*, p. 213.

p. 73, par. 3, Michael Shapiro, *The Jewish 100: A Ranking of the Most Influential Jews of All Time* (New York: Citadel Press, 2000), p. 174. (In a list that starts with Moses at number one, Golda Meir is ranked number forty-five.)

CHAPTER 8

p. 80, Elihu Agress, *Golda Meir: Portrait of a Prime Minister* (New York: Sabra Books, 1969), p. 58.

p. 81, Agress, p. 6.

p. 82, Robert Slater, *Golda, the Uncrowned Queen of Israel* (Middle Village, NY: Jonathan David, 1981), p. 142.

p. 85, *My Life*, p. 313.

CHAPTER 9

p. 89, par. 2, *My Life*, p. 104.

p. 90, par. 4, Agress, p. 132.

p. 91, par. 1, Julia Baird, "The Pursuit of Power Isn't Pretty," *Newsweek*, March 17, 2008.

p. 91, par. 2, *My Life*, pp. 378–79.

CHAPTER 10

p. 93, par. 1, Burkett, p. 6.

p. 94, Quoted in *My Life*, p. 384.

p. 97, *My Life*, p. 425.

p. 98, par. 2, *My Life*, p. 438.

p. 98-99, par. 5, American Presidency Project, University of California, Santa Barbara, online at www.presidency.ucsb.edu

CHAPTER 11

p. 101, Amos Elton, "My Life." *New York Times*, November 30, 1975.

p. 102, par. 1, *New York Theatre Wire*, reviewed November 5, 2003. www.nytheatre-wire.com

p. 102-03, par. 3-par. 1, "Remarks by Golda Meir to President Sadat in the Knesset" www.jewishvirtuallibrary.org

FURTHER INFORMATION

BOOKS

Luxenberg, Alan H. *The Palestine Mandate and the Creation of Israel, 1920–1949*. Broomall, PA: Mason Crest Publishers, 2007.

Reich, Bernard. *A Brief History of Israel*. New York: Checkmark Books, 2008.

Sofer, Barbara. *Keeping Israel Safe: Serving in the Israel Defense Forces*. Minneapolis: Kar-Ben Publishing, 2008.

Wool, Daniel. *Judaism*. New York: Marshall Cavendish, 2007.

DVDS

Against All Odds: Israel Survives: The Complete First Season. Questar, 2006.

Elusive Peace: Israel and the Arabs. PBS Home Video, 2006.

Exodus. 1960 movie starring Paul Newman. MGM, 2002.

Israel: A Nation Is Born. Homevision, 2002.

Israel: Birth of a Nation. The History Channel, 2005.

WEBSITES

Virtual Jewish Library
A project of the American-Israeli Cooperative Enterprise.
www.jewishvirtuallibrary.org

Palestine Facts
A similar site from the Palestinian point of view.
www.palestinefacts.org

BIBLIOGRAPHY

BOOKS

Agress, Elijahu. *Golda Meir: Portrait of a Prime Minister.* New York: Sabra Books, 1969.

Ben-Gurion, David. *Days of David Ben-Gurion.* New York: Grossman Publishers, 1967.

——. *Israel: A Personal History.* New York: Funk & Wagnalls, 1961.

Burkett, Elinor. *Golda.* New York: HarperCollins, 2008.

Chapman, Colin. *Whose Promised Land? The Continuing Crisis over Israel and Palestine.* Grand Rapids, MI: Baker Books, 2002.

Martin, Ralph G. *Golda: The Romantic Years.* New York: Scribner, 1988.

Meir, Golda. *My Life.* New York: Putnam, 1975.

Reinharz, Shulamit, and Mark A. Raider. *American Jewish Women and the Zionist Enterprise.* Hanover, NH: UPNE, 2005.

Shapiro, Michael. *The Jewish 100: A Ranking of the Most Influential Jews of All Time.* New York: Citadel Press, 2000.

Slater, Robert. *Golda, the Uncrowned Queen of Israel.* Middle Village, NY: Jonathan David, 1981.

Syrkin, Marie. *Golda Meir: Israel's Leader.* New York: Putnam, 1969.

PERIODICALS

Baird, Julia. "The Pursuit of Power Isn't Pretty." *Newsweek,* March 17, 2008.

"Brits thought Golda honest, earnest and lacking a sense of humor" *Jerusalem Post,* January 7, 1996, p. 12.

Elon, Amos. "My Life." *New York Times,* November 30, 1975.

"Grandmother—Diplomat." *New York Times* July 12, 1968.

Grose, Peter. "The Partition of Palestine 35 Years Ago." *New York Times,* November 21, 1982.

Krosney, Herbert. "How Israel Went to War." *The Nation,* November 5, 1973, pp. 454–56.

Shlaim, Avi. "A Somber Anniversary." *The Nation,* May 26, 2008, pp. 12–16.

"A Talk with Golda Meir," (signed by E.R.F.S.). *New York Times Magazine,* August 27, 1972.

"To millions of admirers around the world, Golda Meir was grandmother to a nation." *Boston Globe,* December 4, 1981.

ONLINE

American Presidency Project, University of California, Santa Barbara, www.presidency.ucsb.edu

"Remarks by Golda Meir to President Sadat in the Knesset." www.jewishvirtuallibrary.org.

Review of "My Life," *New York Theatre Wire,* reviewed November 5, 2003. www.nytheatre-wire.com.

INDEX

Abdullah (king of Jordan), 68
Abraham, 8, **9**, 9
anti-Semitism, 5, 29, 65
Arab countries. *See* Palestinian people;
  specific countries
Arafat, Yasser, 84

Balfour Declaration, 20-21, 30-31, 32-33,
  34
Begin, Menachem, 102, 103
Ben-Gurion, David, 32-33, 61, 98-99
  Golda Meir and, 19-20, 38, **70**
  Histadrut (United Federation of Labor),
    48-49
  Israeli government and, 73, 75, 79, 87
British Mandate, 33, 34-35, 38-39, 56, 62,
  64-65

Camp David Accords, 103
Cossacks, **4**, 5, 6

Dayan, Moshe, 87-88, 99
Dreyfus, Alfred, 29

education, Golda Meir and, 13-14, 15, 16,
  17-18
Egypt, 22, 94-95
  Anwar al-Sadat and, 102-103
  Gamal Abdel Nasser, 80, 84, 95
  wars against Israel and, 72, 76, 80-81,
    88, 96, 97, 98
Eichmann, Adolf, **83**, 83-84
Eshkol, Levi, 87, 90

family life, 87, 101
  childhood and, 7, 11, 14-17
  children and, 41, 45, 47-48
  kibbutzim and, 37-38
  marriage, 15, 20, 21, 42, 77
flag, Israeli, **22**, 30

Gaza, 76, 80, 89
Golan Heights, 85, 89, 96
government, 64-65, 74-75, 87-88
government, Meir's role in
  ambassador to the Soviet Union, 74
  foreign minister, 79-85
  minister of labor, 74-76
  prime minister, 93-99

Yishuv and, 38-39, 42, 44-45, 49,
  51-52, 64-65

Haganah, 53-54, **54**, 60, 64
health problems, 36, 37, 39, 62, 87
Hebrew language, 35, 79
Herzl, Theodor, 28, 29
Histadrut (United Federation of Labor), 48-49,
  55
Holocaust, the, 59, 60-61, **63**

immigration
  after World War II, 62, 64-65, 66-67,
    68-69
  before World War I, 28, 30
  between World Wars, 34, 53, 55-56
  German refugees and, 55-56, 57
  Golda Meir and, 23, 25
  Law of Return and, 76-77
  War of Independence and, 75-76
Israel, 22
  ancient Israel, 8-9, 25-27
  Arab countries and, 80-82, 84-85
  government of, 44-45, 74-75, 87-88, 91
  independence of, 69, 71-72
  United Nations and, 66-69
  wars with Arab countries and, 72-73,
    88-90, 96-99
  World War II and, 59, 61
  See also Palestine; Yishuv

Jerusalem, 41, 43, 72, 88-89
Jordan, 22, 34, 68, 72, 76, 85, 89
Judaism, 5, 6, 8-9

kibbutzim, 19, 32, 35-39, **38**, 47, 62
Knesset, 74-75, 87-88, 91

Labor Zionism, 17, 28, 36, **44**, 45-46, 46-47
Law of Return, 76
Lebanon, 22, 72, 85

Mabovitch, Blume, 7, 11, 13, 14, 15, 18, 41
Mabovitch, Moshe Yitzhak (Morris), 7, 11, 13,
  41
Mabovitch, Sheyna, 7, 11, 13, 15, 16, 25
Mapai political party, 45, 79, 87
marriage, 15, 20, 21, 42, 77
Merhavia Kibbutz, 36-39

Meyerson, Menachem, 41, 47, 87
Meyerson, Morris, 17, 18, 19, **24**, 77
    marriage to, 20, 21, 42
    Merhavia Kibbutz and, 37–38, 39
Meyerson, Sarah, 41, 46, 47, 62, **75**
military forces
    Haganah, 53–54, **54**, 60, 64
    the Six-Day War, 88–90
    War of Independence, 33, 72–73
    Yom Kippur War, 96–97
minister of labor, Golda Meir as, 74–76

name change, 79
Nasser, Gamal Abdel, 80, 84, 95
Nixon, Richard, 93, 94, 97

Ottoman Empire, 20–21, 31, 32

Palestine
    emigrating to, 23, 25
    Jewish settlers, 28, 30, 34, 53, 55–56
    moving to, 19, 20, 23
    partitioning of, 55, 56, 67–68, 69
    proposed Arab nation of, 56, 59
    See also Israel; Yishuv
Palestine Liberation Organization (PLO),
    84–85
Palestinian people
    attacks on Jewish settlers and, 34,
        52–53
    Balfour Declaration and, 31, 34
    general strike and, 54–55
    partitioning of Palestine and, 59,
        67–68, 69
parliamentary system, 74–75
partition, of Palestine, 55, 56, 67–68, 69
peace plans, 76, 95, 97–98, 102–103
Pioneer Women, 45, 46–47
plays, about Golda Meir, 101–102
pogroms, 6, **10**
political parties, 44–45, 79, 87
prime minister, Golda Meir as, 90–91,
    93–99
Proclamation of Independence, 71
public opinion, of Golda Meir, 47, 52, 65,
    99, 101
public speaking, 14, 19, 61, 73, 81–82, 90

Rabin, Yitzhak, 99
refugees, 55–56, 57, 61, 62, 64–65, 66–67
religious beliefs, Judaism and, 8, 9, 26, 43
Resolution 242, 90

Russia
    ambassador to the Soviet Union, 74
    anti-Semitism and, 5, 6
    Arab countries and, 88, 98
    emigration to Palestine and, 28
    Golda's childhood and, 5, 7, 11

Sadat, Anwar al-, 95, 102–103
Sharett, Moshe, 79
Sinai Peninsula, 80–82, 88, 89, 95
socialism, 7, 11, 44–45, 52
Solomon's Temple, 26, **27**
Soviet Union, 74, 88, 98
speaking tours, 45–47
Syria, 22, 34
    attacks on Israel and, 85
    the Six-Day War and, 89
    War of Independence and, 72
    Yom Kippur War and, 96, 97, 98

terrorism, 53–54, 68, 80, 84–85
Timeline, 104–105
Truman, Harry, 62, 71–72

United Nations, 66–69, 81–82, 84, 90,
    95, 98
United States
    emigrating to, 11
    Jewish refugees and, 56, 57
    recognition of Israel and, 71–72
    the Six-Day War and, 88
    tours of, 45–46, 46–47, 93–94
    Yom Kippur War and, 97, 98

War of Independence, 72–73, 76
weapons, Israeli military and, 72–73, 81,
    93, 97
Weizmann, Chaim, 30, 57, 75
West Bank, 76, 89, 102
women leaders, 91, 93
World War I, 18, 20, 30–31, 32, 34
World War II, 51, 55–56, 59–62, 64–65

Yemeni Jews, 76–77
Yiddish language, 35
Yishuv, 41, 44–45, 47, 48–49, 51, 64–65
    See also British Mandate; Palestine
Yom Kippur War, 96–97

Zionism, 7, 16–17, 18–21, 23, 27–28,
    29

ABOUT THE AUTHOR

JEAN F. BLASHFIELD has been a writer of many books—more than 140 of them—on many subjects, from house plants to women's history and even murder. Most recently she has written numerous nonfiction books for young people on such subjects as science, history, biography, and government, because she particularly enjoys making confusing issues less confusing. She was the founding editor of the book department at the company that produced the Dungeons & Dragons™ role-playing game and has created three multi-volume encyclopedias. She lived abroad for several years and made trips to Israel, where she became fascinated by Golda Meir. Blashfield lives in southern Wisconsin, where she raised her son and daughter.